Cool Under Pressure

WARM WITH HUMOR

GEORGE J HATCHER

 CasaHatcherPress

This book can be purchased at over 40,000 bookstores and libraries, including brick-and-mortar stores, online, in print, and digitally, including Apple and Kindle. Casa Hatcher Press is a subsidiary of Pretty Face, Inc., Rancho Mirage, California 92270.

Book and cover designed by Casa Hatcher Press

Cool Under Pressuree,Warm With Humor by George J. Hatcher

ISBN 979-8-9989967–02 (Paperback)

ISBN: 979-8-9989967-5-7 (eBook)

Also By George Hatcher

Mario 1: Woman in Jeopardy

Mario 2: Coming of Age

Mario 3: Risky Business

Mario 4: Free Fall

Mario 5: Afire

Mario 6: Marked

Mario 7: Aftershock

Mario 8: Captivated

Single Titles

One Wilshire

Gabi

Rico

Cats: Meow Is The Language Of Love

HER: Artistic Expressions Through AI

Elegance In White: Through Wedding Gowns

Quinceañera Fashion: Fifteen & Fabulous

Billion Dollar Rainmaker Part I

Pages of Passion Book 1: My First 19 Years

Pages of Passion Book 2: Bold Beginnings

Pages of Passion Book 3: Rising Waves

Pages of Passion Book 4: Threads Of Destiny

Living Fully While We Wait to Die: Mindfulness Amid Mortality

Beyond The Scale: Health Benefits of Keto for Wellness

Love Is What It Is: Lessons From Everyday Life

Coming Soon

Pages of Passion Book 5

Pages of Passion Book 6

Pages of Passion Book 7

Mario 9

Gabi 2

Rico 2

Dedication

Molly,

In the dance of life, you are my steady partner,

and in every melody, you are my cherished harmony.

With enduring love,

George

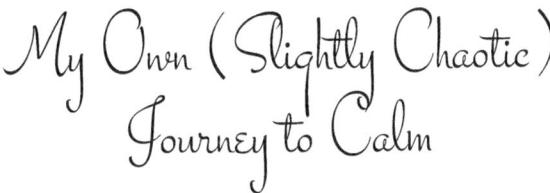

My Own (Slightly Chaotic) Journey to Calm

Let me start by confessing something a little... inconvenient. Writing a book called "Cool Under Pressure, Warm with Humor" is a bit like a cat writing a guide on how to *not* chase laser pointers. I mean, sure, I know the theory, but in practice? My internal monologue often sounds less like serene wisdom and more like a frantic squirrel trying to juggle a thousand acorns while simultaneously filing its taxes.

For years, my natural state could be described as "enthusiastically agitated." My brain operates at roughly 100 miles an hour, which sounds productive, but often translates to:

- **Impatience:** If there's a line, I've already calculated the optimal strategy to cut it (mentally, of course... mostly). If a conversation isn't getting to the point, my inner monologue is screaming, "Just *get there already!*"
- **Verbal Velocity:** This rapid-fire thinking often leads to my mouth engaging before my brain has fully cleared customs. I've said things, oh, *so many things*, that have come across as blunt, dismissive, or even offensive, when my intention was simply to be efficient or, ironically, to help. "Just do X!" comes out, when "Have

you considered X?" would have been far more... *human*. And the immediate internal cringe is usually a tidal wave. *Why did I say that? Now they probably think I'm a monster!* (See? There's that self-talk doing its thing, too).

• **The Pursuit of Perfection (and Panic When It Doesn't Happen):** I'm the person who can plan a complex project down to the nanosecond, and if one tiny cog goes off course, my internal alarm bells go off like a fire drill in a clown college. Calm? Cool? Collected? In those moments, I'm more akin to a slightly melting ice cube in a very hot sauna.

So, why am *I* writing this book? Precisely *because* I've had to learn these lessons the hard way. This isn't theoretical advice from some perfectly serene guru who floats through life on a cloud of chamomile tea. This is a battle-tested guide from someone who *gets it*. Someone who knows what it's like to feel your blood pressure rise because the Wi-Fi is slow, or to replay an awkward conversation for three days straight, wishing you had a "rewind" button for your mouth.

This book is less about achieving monastic calm and more about finding your own personal brand of "cool." It's about:

• **Taming that inner chatter:** Not silencing it entirely (that's unrealistic!), but transforming it from a nagging critic into your most hilarious and supportive cheerleader.

• **Learning to pause:** Just long enough to ensure your words build bridges, not burn them, especially when your impatience is revving its engine.

• **Embracing the glorious mess that is you:** Because perfection is a myth, and true composure often comes from acknowledging your quirks and laughing along with them.

Consider this your backstage pass to transforming your internal monologue, not into a boring lecture, but into a stand-up comedy routine where you're the star, and the punchlines are all about empowerment. We'll explore practical strategies, laugh at our shared human foibles, and discover that being "cool under pressure" doesn't mean being emotionless; it means being **Cool Under Pressure, Warm with Humor.**

Let's dive in, shall we? And trust me, I'm right there with you, probably muttering a positive affirmation under my breath as I type this.

Part 1: Why Self-Talk Matters (And Why You Should Care)

The Voice in Your Head: Friend or Foe?

The voice in your head can often feel like that overly chatty coworker who just can't take a hint. You know, the one who keeps reminding you of every mistake you've ever made, especially when you're trying to focus on a big presentation or, in my case, trying desperately *not* to say something blunt and regrettable. It chirps away, offering unsolicited commentary like, "Remember that time you tripped over your own shoelaces during the meeting? Classic!" Or, my personal favorite: "Oh, you just said *that*? They're probably thinking you're incredibly rude right now. Good job, genius."

What is Self-Talk, Anyway?

Before we dive deeper, let's quickly define what we're even talking about. **Self-talk** is simply that internal monologue, the non-stop stream of thoughts that runs through your mind all day long. It's the way you communicate with yourself, whether you're aware of it or not.

For example:

- You're running late, and you think: "Ugh, I'm so disorganized. I'll never get there on time, and everyone will judge me." (Negative self-talk)
- You just aced a presentation, and you think: "Wow, I really nailed that! I felt confident and clear." (Positive self-talk)
- You're trying to figure out a new gadget, and you mutter to yourself: "Okay, first I plug this in, then I find the power button. This shouldn't be too hard." (Instructional/Neutral self-talk)
- *My version, when impatiently waiting for something:* "Seriously? How hard can it be? Just press the button! Is this person

operating on dial-up internet? C'mon, c'mon, c'mon!" (Agitated self-talk, often leading to outwardly visible impatience or a regrettable sigh).

It's this constant internal chatter that shapes our emotions, our reactions, and ultimately, our reality. And for someone like me, whose default setting can sometimes be "on edge," understanding and redirecting this voice has been a game-changer – a slow, often comical, game-changer, but a game-changer nonetheless.

But what if, instead of a nagging presence, you could turn this internal monologue into your own personal cheerleader? It might be time to upgrade that mental playlist from "The Greatest Hits of Your Worst Moments" to "You Got This, Superstar!"

Let's face it, we've all had that moment where the voice in our head becomes a dramatic critic, clutching its invisible pearls and gasping at your every decision. You send an email and immediately hear, "Oh no, did I forget to attach the report? They'll think I'm a total amateur!" Spoiler alert: They probably won't. Most people are too busy worrying about their own emails to critique yours with a magnifying glass. Instead of letting your inner critic run wild, try flipping the script. Next time that voice pipes up, throw in a "But I did remember to say 'thank you'—that's a win!" and watch it sputter in confusion.

Now, let's not ignore the fact that sometimes that voice can actually be a decent advisor, albeit one that needs a good dose of humor. Maybe it's wise to remind yourself of past pitfalls, but there's a fine line between constructive criticism and a full-blown roast session. Picture your inner dialogue as a conversation with a friend who's kind but has a penchant for sarcasm. Instead of saying, "You'll mess this up," how about it says, "Hey, remember the last time you thought you'd mess it up? You crushed it! Let's do that again." That's the kind of banter we all need—a mix of encouragement and a lighthearted jab.

However, we must acknowledge that sometimes, this internal voice can turn into a real party pooper, throwing cold water on your enthusiasm. You walk into a networking event feeling like a million bucks, only for that voice to say, "What if everyone thinks you're awkward?" Well, guess what? You might be awkward! But you're also charming, and people love a good story—especially the one where you hilariously fumble your way through an introduction. Embrace the awkwardness; it's what makes you relatable. So, the next time that voice tries to rain on your parade, just don your metaphorical sunglasses and strut through the storm with a smile.

In the grand scheme of things, the voice in your head doesn't have to be a foe. With a little practice, it can become your most loyal sidekick. Transforming that inner critic into a supportive friend requires a sprinkle of humor and a dash of self-compassion. After all, life is too short to let that voice run the show. So, the next time you hear it chime in with negativity, remind yourself, "I'm the star of this show, and I'll take constructive feedback, but I'll also throw in a few punchlines!" And just like that, you'll be cool, calm, and collected, ready to tackle whatever comes your way.

The Science of Self-Talk

The Science of Self-Talk: It's Not Just You (And Your Brain is Doing Some Weird Stuff)

Self-talk is that invisible dialogue we engage in throughout our day, and let's face it, if you're anything like the average person (or, ahem, me), you've probably had a conversation with yourself that would make anyone question your sanity. You know, those moments when you're stuck in traffic and suddenly become the world's leading expert on why the person in front of you is driving at a snail's pace? Welcome to the Science of Self-Talk, where you're not just talking to yourself; you're also doing some serious mental gymnastics that would make even the most seasoned acrobat dizzy.

The beauty of self-talk is that it's a universal experience. Whether you're a high-powered executive who can recall last quarter's sales figures with frightening precision, or someone who can't remember where they parked their car after a grocery run (guilty as charged, on most days), we all have our inner monologues. This internal chatter can range from the motivational pep talks we give ourselves before a big meeting ("You've got this, don't forget the key points!") to the self-deprecating remarks that pop up when we drop our lunch on the floor ("Classic! I can't even hold a sandwich, how do I expect to run a meeting?"). Science has shown that these inner dialogues can significantly affect our mood, performance, and even our physical well-being. So, the next time you catch yourself muttering about how you'll never succeed because you can't even fold a fitted sheet, remember that you're in good company. Your brain is just being... well, your brain.

Now, let's talk about some of the wild and wacky ways our brains engage in self-talk, often without us even realizing it. Think of your brain as a super-fast, slightly eccentric, information processor. It loves shortcuts. It loves patterns. And sometimes, these shortcuts lead to what scientists call **cognitive distortions**. Sounds fancy, right? Really, they're just polite terms for "mental habits that make you feel worse than you need to."

Meet the Brain's Favorite Pranksters: Cognitive Distortions

These aren't rare psychological ailments; they're the everyday mental hiccups that skew our self-talk towards the negative. Let's introduce a few of the most common ones – you'll probably recognize some of these little rascals:

• **All-or-Nothing Thinking (The Drama Queen):** This is when your self-talk sees everything in black and white, no shades of gray. You either nail it perfectly, or you're a complete failure. "I forgot one minor detail in that presentation; I completely bombed it!" There's no room for "I did well overall, but learned to double-check next time." My own impatience often fuels this: if something isn't instantly perfect, my brain yells, "It's ruined! Just give up!" It's quite the show.

• **Overgeneralization (The Fortune Teller of Doom):** One bad experience, and your self-talk predicts a lifetime of similar misery. You trip on the stairs once, and your inner voice immediately declares, "I'm such a clumsy person! I'll probably trip every time I walk up stairs now and end up in a full-body cast!" One awkward conversation, and suddenly, "I'm terrible at networking.

I'll never make new connections." Your brain sees a single molehill and immediately constructs a mountain range of perpetual failure.

• **Catastrophizing (The Sky-Is-Falling Prophet):** This is when your self-talk takes a small problem and blows it up into a looming disaster of epic proportions. Your boss sends an email asking to chat, and your inner voice immediately jumps to: "Oh no, I'm going to be fired! I'll lose my house! I'll end up living in a cardboard box under a bridge, forced to knit sweaters for stray cats!" All because of a meeting request. My impatient brain takes this to eleven: a tiny delay means utter ruination.

• **Mental Filter (The Negative Spotlight):** Your brain wears cynical glasses, focusing only on the negative details while ignoring all the positives. You get ten positive comments on a project and one constructive critique, and your self-talk fixates solely on that one critique. "They hated it. That one person said the font was off; clearly, the whole thing is a disaster." It's like going to a fantastic concert but only remembering the one slightly off-key note.

Understanding these little "pranksters" is the first step to hijacking their power. When you can identify them, you can start to argue back, or better yet, laugh them into submission. Because here's the kicker: the research, from fields like cognitive behavioral therapy (CBT) to positive psychology, overwhelmingly supports the idea that **what you tell yourself profoundly impacts how you feel and perform.** Your thoughts aren't just fleeting wisps; they're the architects of your emotional landscape.

Now, let's talk about the role of humor in self-talk. You might find yourself in a stressful work situation, and instead of panicking, you can choose to laugh at the absurdity of it all. Imagine standing in front of your team, realizing you've just mispronounced the name of your biggest client. Instead of cringing and letting the "All-or-Nothing Thinker" declare you a professional fraud, you could quip, "Well, at least I'm not their worst nightmare—just their slightly confused acquaintance who occasionally mangles names!" This kind of lightheartedness not only alleviates tension but also fosters a more positive mindset. The science backs it up: laughter releases endorphins, those delightful little chemicals that make you feel good, which can make your self-talk more empowering and help to rewrite those negative neural pathways. It's like giving your brain a delightful, neurochemical spa day.

But let's not forget the power of positive affirmations. You might be rolling your eyes right now, thinking they're just for yoga classes and motivational posters, but hear me out. Research shows that repeating positive affirmations can actually help rewire your brain by strengthening new, positive neural connections. It's like paving a new, smoother mental highway instead of constantly taking the old, bumpy, pothole-filled road of negative self-talk. So, instead of telling yourself, "I'm never going to get that promotion because I'm clearly a walking disaster," try "I'm a powerhouse of potential, and my boss is just waiting for me to shine!" It might feel a bit silly at first, just like that awkward dance move you tried at your cousin's wedding, but it can become second nature with practice. Plus, who doesn't want to feel like a superhero in their own life story, even if you're still trying to figure out how to put on the cape without tripping?

In the grand scheme of things, self-talk is not just a quirky habit; it's a vital tool for success. Understanding the science behind it can help business people, professionals, and everyday folks harness the power of their words—both spoken and unspoken. So, the next time you find yourself talking to yourself, remember: it's not just you. Your brain is a complex, hilarious, and sometimes mischievous entity. Embrace the humor, sprinkle in some positive affirmations, and watch as your inner dialogue transforms from a mere whisper to a powerful roar. After all, if you're going to talk to yourself, you might as well make it a conversation worth having!

Pause & Ponder: Your Inner Voice Audit

Let's get curious about your own inner voice. For the next day or two, simply *notice* your self-talk. Don't judge it, just observe.

- **What are its dominant themes?** Is it mostly critical? Worried? Encouraging? Sarcastic?
- **Does it tend to fall into any of the "prankster" categories** (All-or-Nothing, Overgeneralization, Catastrophizing, Mental Filter)?
- **When is your self-talk most negative?** (e.g., first thing in the morning, under pressure, when you're tired, after a mistake).
- **When is it most positive?**

Just becoming aware is a huge step. You might even want to give your inner voice a funny nickname based on its dominant personality (e.g., "Brenda the Buzkill," "Captain Catastrophe," or "Cheerleader Charlie"). This helps you externalize it and realize it's not *you*, but a part of your brain's operating system that can be updated.

The Power of Positive Affirmations

~~~~

Affirmations: Like Magic But Without the Wand (More Like a Really Good Espresso Shot for Your Brain)

Imagine if you could wave a magic wand and *poof!* Instant confidence, unwavering focus, and the ability to charm your way through any business meeting. While we may not have access to Hogwarts (or even a reliable teleportation device for those morning commutes), we do have affirmations—those snazzy little phrases that can transform our mindset faster than you can say, "Where's my coffee?" Think of affirmations as the self-help equivalent of a good cup of espresso: they can perk you up, boost your mood, and help you tackle the day without feeling like you've just hit the snooze button for the fifth time.

Let's face it, the modern business world can feel like a high-stakes game of poker where everyone is bluffing their way through. You walk into a meeting, and suddenly it feels like everyone else is holding a royal flush while you're clutching a pair of twos. Enter affirmations: your secret weapon against the imposter syndrome lurking in the shadows. Instead of letting that internal voice tell you you're not good enough (a favorite trick of our "All-or-Nothing Thinker" friend, as we learned!), you can replace it with a simple phrase like "I am capable and confident." Just saying it a few times can make you feel like you're wearing an invisible cape—one that says, "I've got this!"

But wait, these aren't just empty words. The real magic happens when you understand the *types* of affirmations and how they interact with your brain.

Beyond "I Am": Different Flavors of Affirmations

While "I am confident" is a great start, affirmations come in a few delicious flavors, each designed to boost a different aspect of your mental game:

1 "I Am" Affirmations (The Power Declaration): These focus on your identity and who you are becoming. They're about declaring your inherent worth and capabilities.

◦ *Examples:* "I am resilient and resourceful." "I am a calm and clear communicator." "I am capable of handling any challenge."

2 "I Choose" Affirmations (The Control Button): These are fantastic for when you feel overwhelmed or stuck. They remind you that you have agency and can make conscious decisions about your state of mind.

◦ *Examples:* "I choose to remain calm in stressful situations." "I choose to focus on solutions, not problems." "I choose to see challenges as opportunities for growth."

3 "I Have" Affirmations (The Gratitude Booster): These focus on what you possess, whether it's skills, opportunities, or positive traits. They help shift your mindset to abundance.

◦ *Examples:* "I have the knowledge to succeed." "I have a supportive network around me." "I have endless creativity to draw upon."

4 Process-Oriented Affirmations (The Action Plan): These are brilliant for goals, as they focus on the actions you're taking or the person you're *being* to achieve them.

◦ *Examples:* "I am consistently taking steps towards my goals."

"I am learning and growing every day." "I am effectively managing my time and energy."

The trick is not just *saying* the words, but trying to *feel* them as you say them. Imagine the sensation of confidence, the feeling of calm. It's like your brain is a sophisticated sound system, and affirmations are the specific frequency you want to tune into. The more you play that station, the clearer the signal becomes.

Now, you might be wondering how to incorporate these magical phrases into your daily routine without looking like you're auditioning for a role in a cheesy infomercial. Fear not! You can sprinkle affirmations into your life like confetti at a birthday party. Start your day by saying them in front of the mirror (yes, it feels a bit odd at first, like having a serious conversation with your reflection, but trust me, it works), or whisper them under your breath during that awkward elevator ride with your boss. Just keep it subtle; no one wants to be the person who accidentally yells, "I am the master of my destiny!" while everyone else is trying to enjoy their coffee in peace. Though, if you *do* try that, please send me the hilarious outcome.

And let's not forget about the power of repetition. You've probably heard that it takes 21 days to form a habit, but let's be real: it might take a few more days when you're trying to convince your brain that you're a rock star, especially when your inner critic (that "Catastrophizing" character) is busy predicting your imminent downfall. The trick is to keep it light and fun. Create a mantra that makes you chuckle, like "I'm a business wizard—watch me conjure up success while simultaneously keeping my plants alive!" By keeping it humorous, you'll not only be more likely to remember it, but you'll also feel less like you're forcing yourself to engage in a self-help seminar. You want to empower yourself, not put yourself to sleep!

Common Affirmation Pitfalls (and How to Avoid Them with a Smile):

Sometimes people try affirmations and say, "They didn't work!" Often, it's because of these common hiccups:

• **Being Too Vague:** "I am good" is nice, but "I am a skilled problem-solver who approaches challenges with creative solutions" is far more impactful. Be specific!

• **Not Believing It (Yet):** If you say "I am a millionaire" when your bank account disagrees, your brain's "BS detector" will likely kick in. Start with something you can *almost* believe, or phrase it as a desire: "I am open to attracting financial abundance" or "I am building wealth step-by-step." Remember, it's a journey, not a magic instant transformation.

• **Focusing on What You DON'T Want:** Affirmations should be positive. Instead of "I am not anxious," try "I am calm and composed." Your brain struggles to process negatives.

• **Giving Up Too Soon:** Just like learning to ride a bike, you'll wobble. The key is to keep pedaling. Consistency over perfection, always.

So, the next time you feel the pressure mounting—whether it's a looming deadline, a challenging presentation, or just the existential dread of another Monday morning (I feel you on that one, trust me)—remember that affirmations can work wonders. They may not be magic wands, but they're pretty darn close. Embrace them, laugh a little, and watch as they transform your self-talk from a timid whisper into a triumphant roar. Because in the grand circus of life and business, you deserve to be the ringmaster, not just another clown juggling stress.

Pause & Ponder: Your Affirmation Exploration

1 Identify a current area of challenge or a quality you want to cultivate. (e.g., public speaking, handling criticism, patience, creativity).

2 Draft 2-3 affirmations using different "flavors" (e.g., "I Am," "I Choose," "I Have," or Process-Oriented).

◦ *Example for impatience:* "I am patient and grounded, even when things move slowly." "I choose to breathe deeply before react-ing." "I am learning to embrace the pause."

3 Say them out loud. Do they feel good? Do they make you crack a smile? Tweak them until they resonate and feel genuinely *yours*.

4 Pick one to try for the next 24 hours. Whisper it, think it, write it down. See how it subtly shifts your inner landscape.

Crafting Your Affirmation: Make It Yours, Not a Hallmark Card (Unless Aunt Edna's Cat is a Super CEO)

When it comes to crafting your affirmation, the first rule is to keep it personal. You're not writing a generic Hallmark card for your Aunt Edna's cat's birthday; you're creating a powerful mantra that speaks directly to your own life, quirks, and aspirations. So, ditch the generic "I am great" nonsense and get specific. Instead of saying, "I am successful," try something like, "I'm the kind of person who can sell ice to an Eskimo while keeping a straight face and probably getting a laugh out of them." Or, for someone like me, who battles impatience, perhaps: "I am a master of the pause, embracing moments of stillness even when my brain wants to run a marathon." Make it resonate with your unique experiences, skills, and maybe even your inside jokes. This is *your* affirmation, not a one-size-fits-all sweater that shrinks in the wash.

Next, let's inject a little humor into your affirmation. Life is already a circus, so why not throw in a few laughs? Humor isn't just about entertainment; it's a powerful deflector shield against negativity and self-doubt. When you laugh, your brain releases those wonderful endorphins we talked about, instantly shifting your mood. So, instead of saying, "I am calm under pressure," you could say, "I'm as calm as a cat in a sunbeam, even when my to-do list looks like a novel written by a hyperactive octopus." Or, if you're like me and your mind races: "My thoughts are like a herd of wild horses, but I'm the cowboy who can always wrangle them back into the corral (eventually!)." Humor not only makes your affirmation more memorable but also helps to lighten the mood in stressful situations. After all, who wants to sound like a motivational poster when you can sound like the star of your own comedy show? A little chuckle can go a long way in boosting your confidence when the pressure is on.

Remember, an affirmation needs to be **actionable**, or at least imply action. It's not enough to simply declare your awesomeness; you must also back it up with a sense of purpose or a subtle nudge towards behavior. Instead of, "I am a great leader," consider, "I am a great leader who delegates tasks like a pro and doesn't micromanage like a controlling helicopter parent, unless it's *really* important, then maybe just a little hovering." This version not only defines what you want to be but also outlines the behaviors that will get you there. Affirmations should serve as a roadmap to your success, guiding you away from the pitfalls of procrastination and towards the land of productivity. Think of them as tiny, empowering GPS instructions for your brain.

Let's talk about the power of repetition. Just like that annoying jingle you can't seem to shake off (hello, catchy commercial tunes!), your affirmation should stick in your mind. Repeat it daily, but do it in a way that doesn't feel like a chore. Consider incorporating it into your morning routine, perhaps while you brush your teeth or dance around in your pajamas (a personal favorite, though my dog remains unimpressed). You can whisper it to yourself during your coffee break, or write it on a sticky note and put it somewhere you'll see it often. When you make your affirmation a regular part of your day, you're not just saying it; you're living it. And who knows? You might just find yourself busting out a few dance moves along the way, which is a great stress reliever. Consistency is the secret sauce here; it's less about a grand performance and more about tiny, regular nudges.

Finally, give yourself permission to **evolve your affirmation**. Just like your fashion sense, your needs and goals will change over time. What worked for you last year might feel as outdated as a flip phone today. So, don't hesitate to tweak or completely overhaul your affirmations as you grow. If you find yourself in a new job or pursuing a different passion, adjust your words to reflect this new chapter. Remember, the only constant in life is change, and your affirmations should be as flexible as your yoga instructor (or a slinky, depending on your preferred metaphor). So, go ahead and make it yours—after all, there's no Hallmark card that can truly capture the essence of your unique journey.

Pause & Ponder: Your Personal Affirmation Lab

Time to roll up your sleeves and get experimental!

1 Identify a specific challenge or goal: What's one thing you want to feel more calm, cool, or collected about right now? (e.g., handling unexpected changes, speaking up in meetings, managing a specific difficult person, being more patient).

2 Brainstorm keywords: What words make you feel strong, capable, or humorous in relation to this challenge? (e.g., "flow," "grace," "quick wit," "unflappable," "master," "ninja").

3 Draft a humorous, actionable affirmation: Combine your keywords into a statement. Try to make it personal and, if possible, elicit a small chuckle.

◦ *If your challenge is impatience, you might try:* "I am a Zen master of waiting, finding peace even when the line moves slower than a snail on tranquilizers."

◦ *If it's handling criticism:* "I absorb feedback like a sponge, then wring out the negativity and use the good bits to sparkle."

◦ *If it's feeling overwhelmed:* "I am the conductor of my own chaos, turning symphony of stress into a rock opera of awesome."

4 Test drive it: Say it out loud. Does it feel good? Does it make you crack a smile? Tweak them until they resonate and feel genuinely *yours*.

Cool, Calm, and Collected: The Art of Composure

Breathing Techniques: Inhale Confidence, Exhale Doubt (It's Like a Mini Vacation for Your Lungs and Brain)

Breathing techniques are like the secret sauce in the recipe of life; they can turn a bland day into a gourmet experience. Imagine this: you're in a meeting, and your boss just asked you to present your latest project. Your heart starts racing, palms are sweaty, and the only thing you can think of is how much you'd rather be at home binge-watching your favorite series. For someone like me, with an impatience meter that often hits "critical," this is precisely when my internal voice starts screaming: "Oh no, oh no, oh no! Why me?! Just get it over with already!"

But wait! Instead of spiraling into a mini panic attack, you can inhale confidence and exhale doubt. Sounds easy, right? Well, it is —if you know how to breathe like a pro. This isn't about just *surviving*; it's about giving your nervous system a gentle, yet firm, pep talk.

First things first, let's get acquainted with the art of deep breathing. You might be thinking, "I breathe every day; what's the big deal?" Well, my friend, there's a difference between the kind of breathing that keeps you alive (the automatic, shallow kind) and the kind that sets your inner Zen master free. The latter actively tells your body, "Hey, we're not running from a saber-toothed tiger right now. Chill." This message is sent via the **vagus nerve**, a kind of superhighway between your brain and your major organs. Deep, slow breathing stimulates this nerve, flipping your body from "fight-or-flight" into "rest-and-digest" mode.

Picture yourself inhaling deeply through your nose, filling your lungs like a balloon at a birthday party, letting your belly expand. Then, exhale slowly through your mouth, as if you're trying to blow out a candle without burning your eyebrows off. This technique not only calms those jittery nerves but also sends a message to your brain that you're in control—like a boss, but without the need for a tie (or the urge to tap your foot impatiently).

Your Calm-Inducing Breathing Menu: Choose Your Flavor!

While any deep breathing is good, here are a couple of specific techniques you can deploy when you need to activate your inner cool:

1 Box Breathing (The Four-Sided Fix): This one is fantastic because it's so structured, giving your racing mind something concrete to focus on. Imagine drawing a square with your breath.

° **Inhale:** Slowly for 4 counts. (Draw the first side of the box up.)

° **Hold:** Your breath for 4 counts. (Draw the top side across.)

° **Exhale:** Slowly for 4 counts. (Draw the second side down.)

° **Hold:** Your breath again for 4 counts. (Draw the bottom side across, connecting back.)

° My personal twist: As I inhale, I might think, "Inhaling Calm." As I hold, "Holding Patience." As I exhale, "Exhaling Annoyance." As I hold again, "Ready to Roll." It's like a tiny, secret mental choreography.

This technique is a favorite of Navy SEALs for staying calm under extreme pressure. If it works for them in a firefight, it can definitely help you with that demanding client call.

2 4-7-8 Breathing (The Sleepy Time Secret, Also Good for Meetings): Developed by Dr. Andrew Weil, this one is often recommended for sleep, but it's equally powerful for calming anxiety and grounding yourself quickly.

- **Exhale Completely:** Make a "whoosh" sound through your mouth. (Get all that stale anxiety out!)
- **Inhale:** Silently through your nose for a count of 4.
- **Hold:** Your breath for a count of 7.
- **Exhale:** Completely through your mouth, making that "whoosh" sound, for a count of 8.
- Repeat this cycle three more times for a total of four breaths. The longer exhale helps you release tension. Don't worry if you can't hit the exact counts at first; just focus on the ratio. It's about letting go.

Now, let's talk about the power of affirmations while you're at it. As you inhale confidence, you might want to whisper sweet nothings to yourself, like "I am a powerhouse of productivity" or "I could sell ice to an Eskimo (and probably get them to buy a second one on principle)." The key is to make these affirmations so outrageous or personally funny that even your inner critic would raise an eyebrow. Picture it: you're inhaling confidence and exhaling doubt, all while declaring to the universe that you're basically the superhero of your office. Who wouldn't want to channel their inner superhero during a high-stakes presentation?

But wait, there's more! Breathing techniques can be your best friend in social situations too. Imagine walking into a networking event where everyone seems to know each other, and you're feeling that familiar flutter of social awkwardness. My impatient brain often urges me to just barge in or worse, flee. But instead, you could either stand in the corner, awkwardly clutching your drink like it's a life raft, or you could employ your newfound breathing prowess. Inhale confidence, exhale doubt, and suddenly you're the life of the party, charming everyone with your brilliant jokes and engaging stories. Just be careful not to use your deep breathing as a way to talk yourself into believing you can juggle flaming swords while reciting Shakespeare. Trust me, that's not a good look, and it's definitely *not* what I meant by "cool under pressure."

Finally, let's wrap it up with a reminder: breathing techniques aren't just for those high-pressure moments. They're your trusty sidekick in everyday life, whether you're dealing with a demanding client, navigating office politics, or simply trying to find your car keys when you're already late (a common scenario for me, leading to much internal gnashing of teeth). So the next time you feel that familiar flutter of doubt or surge of impatience in your stomach, take a moment to breathe. Inhale confidence, exhale doubt, and remember that you've got this. And if all else fails, just remember to add a sprinkle of humor to your self-talk; after all, laughter is the best medicine—even if it's just for dealing with your own ridiculousness, like the time I nearly tried box breathing while parallel parking. (Do not recommend. Focus on the parking).

Pause & Ponder: Your Breath Blueprint

1 Your Go-To Breath: Try practicing Box Breathing and 4-7-8 Breathing a few times. Which one feels more natural or effective for *you*? You don't have to master both, just find the one that resonates.

2 Trigger Test: Think of one common, low-stakes situation that usually makes you impatient or stressed (e.g., waiting in line, slow internet, a delayed response). For the next day, try to use your chosen breathing technique for just 1-2 minutes when you encounter that trigger.

3 Affirmation Combo: Pair your breathing with a simple affirmation. As you inhale, think your positive affirmation. As you exhale, release the negative thought or feeling.

○ *Example:* Inhale: "I am patient." Exhale: "Releasing urgency."

The Zen of Multitasking: Spoiler Alert—It's a Myth (And Your Brain is Quietly Judging Your Attempts)

In the grand theater of modern life, multitasking often takes center stage, dazzling us with its promise of unparalleled productivity. Picture this: you're in a meeting, responding to emails, and simultaneously brainstorming ideas for your upcoming presentation. You feel like a superhero, wielding the power of multitasking. Spoiler alert: you're really just a juggler with too many flaming torches, and at least three of them are on fire in your hair. The truth is, while our brains might *feel* equipped with a shiny multitasking sticker, they function more like a single-threaded computer than a high-performance server. They do one thing really, really well, and then they quickly (and usually quite inefficiently) switch to the next thing. So, let's take a comedic jaunt into the myth of multitasking and why it might just be the ultimate productivity prank our modern world has played on us.

First off, let's talk about the "superhuman" idea that multitasking helps us get more done. Ever tried cooking dinner while helping your kid with their homework, only to end up with a scorched saucepan and a child who believes math is an ancient language? Or, in my case, trying to answer an urgent email while listening to a podcast and sketching out a new idea, only to realize I've typed gibberish, missed half the podcast, and my sketch looks like a demented potato? Yeah, that's your brain on multitasking.

Research actually shows that switching between tasks can lead to a significant drop in productivity—some studies suggest as much as a 40% decrease in efficiency and an increase in errors. This is due to something called **"attention residue."** When you switch from Task A to Task B, your attention doesn't instantly snap back. A "residue" of your attention lingers on Task A, making it harder to fully engage with Task B. It's like leaving a tiny mental browser tab open in the background, constantly sipping away at your brain's processing power. So the next time you think you're being efficient by answering calls while drafting reports, remember that you're only one coffee spill away from a chaotic disaster, and your brain is quietly tut-tutting your efforts.

Now, let's not forget about the glorious world of self-talk. You might find yourself whispering affirmations like "I can do it all!" or "I'm a multitasking maestro!" But what if I told you that your inner critic is just waiting for you to trip over your own two feet? Every time you switch gears, your brain has to recalibrate, and in that moment of confusion, your self-talk might morph from "I've got this!" to "What have I done to deserve this level of chaos?!" Embrace the irony: the more you try to juggle, the more likely you are to drop the ball—quite literally, if you're not careful. My own impatience used to convince me that doing *everything* at once was the fastest route to completion. Turns out, it was just the fastest route to feeling frazzled and making silly mistakes.

What's the antidote to this multitasking madness, you ask? Enter the art of **single-tasking**, where you dive deep into one task at a time. Think of it as the Zen garden of productivity, or perhaps, a focused laser beam rather than a scattered disco ball. You rake the sand, place your rocks, and feel the tranquility wash over you. In this serene state, you're not just crossing items off your to-do list; you're actually enjoying the process, and doing it *better*. You'll find that your self-talk shifts from frantic phrases like "I'm behind!" to "I'm present and crushing this!" It's like going from a chaotic circus act to a peaceful stroll through the park, and trust me, your brain (and your blood pressure) will thank you for the break.

Practical Strategies for Becoming a Single-Tasking Ninja (with a Smile):

• **The Pomodoro Technique (The Time-Block Tango):** This is a simple but mighty tool. Choose a single task, set a timer for 25 minutes, and work *only* on that task until the timer rings. Then take a 5-minute break. After four "pomodoros," take a longer break (15-30 minutes). It's amazing how much you can accomplish when you commit to one thing for a short, focused burst.

• **Batch Similar Tasks:** Instead of responding to emails whenever they ping, set aside specific "email times" twice a day. Do all your phone calls at one time. Process all your paperwork together. This reduces the mental effort of context switching.

• **Silence the Notifications:** Your phone is a magnificent invention, but it's also a master of distraction. Turn off non-essential notifications during focused work periods. Put your phone on "Do Not Disturb" or even in another room. Your emails can wait. Your social media can *definitely* wait.

• **Clear Your Workspace (and Mind):** A cluttered desk often reflects a cluttered mind. Before starting a single-tasking session, remove anything that isn't directly related to the task at hand. This physical decluttering can lead to mental clarity.

• **Mindful Breaks:** When you take a break, truly take a break. Step away from your screen. Stretch. Look out a window. Grab a glass of water. Don't immediately jump to checking social media, which is just another form of multitasking.

So, as you navigate the whirlwind of business and life, remember that multitasking is more myth than magic. Lean into the humor of it all, and celebrate your escapades in the juggling act of life. By focusing on one thing at a time, you'll discover that being cool under pressure isn't about spinning plates faster; it's about mastering the art of simplicity and deep focus. And while you're at it, give yourself a pat on the back for recognizing the myth —after all, self-talk can be a powerful tool, and a good laugh at our own attempts to be superhuman is the best affirmation of all.

Pause & Ponder: Your Single-Tasking Experiment

1 Identify a Multitasking Hotspot: Where or when do you most often find yourself trying to multitask? (e.g., during meetings, while writing, responding to emails, during family time).

2 Choose One Strategy: Pick one of the single-tasking strategies (Pomodoro, batching, silencing notifications, etc.) to try for just one hour, or for a specific task.

3 Notice the Difference: Pay attention to your self-talk before, during, and after. Did you feel less stressed? More accomplished? Did your brain feel calmer? Even if it felt awkward at first, acknowledge the effort.

4 Laugh About It: If you inevitably slip back into multi-tasking (because we all do!), don't beat yourself up. Just chuckle, say, "Oh, there goes my brain trying to be a superhero again!" and gently redirect yourself.

Turning Negatives into Positives

From "I Can't" to "Watch Me": The Great Transformation (Or, How Your Inner Critic Gets a Hilarious Makeover)

Picture this: You're at a crucial meeting, and the boss drops a bombshell. "We need a presentation on our new strategy by tomorrow!" Panic sets in, and your inner voice starts echoing, "I can't do this. I'm not a magician! I'll probably accidentally delete the whole thing and then spontaneously combust from embarrassment!" This is a classic "Catastrophizing" moment, as we discussed earlier, amplified by a healthy dose of "All-or-Nothing Thinking." My own internal monologue in these situations tends to add: "And there's no way I'll have time for coffee tomorrow! The horror!"

But what if I told you that with a sprinkle of self-talk and a dash of humor, you could transform that "I can't" into a resounding "Watch me!"? It's time to swap the panic for power and embrace the art of self-empowerment. This isn't about ignoring the challenge; it's about shifting your perspective, much like turning a dramatic black-and-white movie into a vibrant, slightly absurd comedy.

Let's face it, we've all been there. That moment when you look at a daunting task and think, "I'd rather wrestle an alligator than tackle this project." Or, more accurately for many of us in the modern world, "I'd rather spend the day organizing my junk drawer than touching that spreadsheet." But here's a thought: what if you approached it like an adventurous game show instead? Change the script in your mind. Instead of saying "I can't," try "I'm about to take on the biggest challenge of my career, and I'm going to make it look fabulous – possibly with jazz hands!" Suddenly, you're not just facing a task; you're auditioning for the role of the confident superstar ready to shine.

The secret sauce to this transformation is positive affirmations and the powerful act of **reframing**. Reframing is like putting a different picture frame around a situation to change how you see it. The picture itself doesn't change, but your perception of it does. So, instead of telling yourself, "I'm terrible at public speaking," how about, "I'm a charismatic speaker who captivates audiences, even if I occasionally stumble over my words like a puppy chasing its tail"? Or, for my own impatience: instead of "I can't believe this is taking so long, I'm going to burst!" I try "This is a great opportunity to practice my Zen master breathing and see how calmly I can ride out this wave of inefficiency." Sure, you might feel like you're auditioning for a role in a soap opera, but who cares? The more you repeat these affirmations and practice reframing, the more your brain starts to believe it. It's like telling yourself you look great in those questionable workout clothes; eventually, you might just strut into the gym like you own the place.

The Power of "Yet": Your Secret Weapon Against "I Can't"

One of the simplest, yet most profound, ways to reframe "I can't" is to add the word "**yet**." This tiny word shifts a fixed mindset (where abilities are static) to a growth mindset (where abilities can be developed).

• Instead of: "I can't understand this new software."

○ Try: "I can't understand this new software **yet**." (Implies you *will* with effort.)

• Instead of: "I'm not good at delegating."

○ Try: "I'm not good at delegating **yet**, but I'm learning to let go of the reins (just a little!)."

• Instead of: "I can't be patient."

○ Try: "I can't be patient **yet**, but I'm practicing slowing down my internal clock one mindful breath at a time."

This single word injects hope, possibility, and a humorous nod to the learning curve of being human.

Now, let's talk about the power of humor in self-talk, especially when reframing. When your inner critic kicks in, imagine that voice is just a quirky character from a sitcom, armed with bad jokes and a penchant for melodrama. You know the type—always overreacting and making mountains out of molehills. Instead of taking it seriously, laugh along! When that voice says, "You'll totally screw this up," you can respond, "Oh, I might! But if I do, at least it'll be a story for the ages, and I'll get some valuable 'lessons learned' for my next comedy set." When you can distance yourself from that negative inner monologue, you'll find it easier to flip the script from "I can't" to "Oh, watch me!" with a wink and a grin. It's not about being naive; it's about being strategically optimistic and resilient.

As you embark on this journey from self-doubt to self-assurance, remember that every great transformation starts with a little courage and a whole lot of humor. Embrace the challenges, channel your inner comedian, and let your self-talk become the empowering mantra that pushes you forward. The next time you find yourself in a tight spot, instead of cringing, smile, take a deep breath, and declare, "Watch me!" You'll not only surprise yourself but also inspire everyone around you to rethink their own "can'ts." After all, isn't it more fun to be a comeback kid with a punchline than a perpetually worried wallflower?

Pause & Ponder: Your Reframing Challenge

1 Your "I Can't" List: Think of 2-3 things you currently tell yourself "I can't" do, or "I'm not good at." Write them down.

◦ *Examples:* "I can't speak up in large meetings." "I'm not good at asking for help." "I can't handle unexpected changes to my schedule."

2 Add "Yet": For each "I can't," simply add "yet" to the end. How does that small word change the feeling?

3 Humorous Reframe: Now, try to reframe each "I can't" into a positive, actionable affirmation that includes a touch of humor. Think about what the *opposite* of that negative thought would look like, and then make it slightly absurd or personally funny.

◦ *Original:* "I can't handle unexpected changes to my schedule."

◦ *Reframe (with humor):* "I am a flexible ninja, gracefully adapting to schedule curveballs even when they surprise me, usually with a dramatic flourish."

4 Practice: Pick one of your reframed affirmations and try to use it the next time that specific "I can't" thought pops into your head. Just notice the shift.

The Compliment Sandwich: How to Serve Your Inner Critic (Even When It's Being a Picky Eater)

Picture this: you're sitting at your desk, yet another email pops up with feedback on your latest project. Your inner critic is already sharpening its knives, ready to slice through your self-esteem like a hot knife through butter. "Oh great, *another* critique," it sneers. "You probably missed something obvious. You always do." This is precisely the moment to reach for your metaphorical apron and assemble the culinary masterpiece of self-talk: **The Compliment Sandwich**.

The Compliment Sandwich allows you to not only survive the critique but thrive in its delicious layers. The key is to wrap your inner critic in a fluffy layer of compliments before diving into the meat of the matter. It's about delivering constructive feedback to yourself (or even to others, but we're focusing on ourselves here!) in a way that's gentle, palatable, and ends on a positive note.

First, let's talk about the **top slice of bread: the Initial Compliment**. You wouldn't serve a sandwich without the bread, right? Start with a compliment that's as genuine as your love for coffee on a Monday morning. This needs to be something you *truly* believe about yourself or your effort.

- "Hey, that report you wrote was insightful and surprisingly concise!"
- "You handled that difficult client call with remarkable patience, even when I (your inner critic) was screaming for you to hang up!"
- "Despite the chaos, you actually managed to get most of your tasks done today. High five!"

Now, whether this is true or not is entirely up to how much coffee you've had that day, but that's the beauty of self-talk. You can sprinkle a little fairy dust over your own achievements and make them shine like a diamond. This first slice of bread sets a positive tone and prepares your inner critic for the juicy filling ahead. It disarms the negativity by acknowledging something good first.

Now, we get to the **meat of the sandwich: The Constructive Criticism**. This is where the honest, but gentle, self-assessment comes in. Don't be afraid to dig into the nitty-gritty, but frame it as an opportunity for growth, not a declaration of failure.

- "However, I think the graphs could use a bit more pizzazz to really grab attention."
- "Next time, I could try taking a few extra deep breaths before responding to diffuse my impatience."
- "It might be helpful to review the project brief one more time to avoid missing minor details."

Ah yes, pizzazz—the magical ingredient that transforms a bland report into a dazzling presentation. Just like adding sprinkles to a cupcake, your inner critic may squirm at first, but it will soon realize that a little constructive feedback isn't the end of the world.

Think of it as seasoning; too much salt is a disaster, but just the right amount elevates the entire dish. This is where you address the "mistake" or the "area for improvement" without letting it swallow your entire self-worth. It's about the action, not about labeling *you* as a failure.

Finally, let's wrap it all up with the **bottom slice of bread: The Reinforcing Compliment**. Finish strong with another genuine compliment to seal the deal. This final layer of bread helps to ensure your inner critic doesn't choke on the meat. It's like a warm hug for your brain, reassuring it that while there may be room for improvement, you're still a rockstar in the grand performance of life.

• "But overall, your attention to detail is impressive, and your dedication truly shines through!"

• "And that kind of mindful pause is exactly the progress we're aiming for, even when my impatience tries to take over."

• "Your ability to get *anything* done today speaks volumes about your resilience."

This technique isn't about being inauthentic or sugarcoating; it's about being strategically kind to yourself. It prevents that common "downward spiral" of negative self-talk where one small mistake snowballs into an all-encompassing belief that you're fundamentally flawed. It teaches your brain to accept feedback without entering full panic mode.

So, the next time your inner critic decides to crash the party, invite it over for a Compliment Sandwich. It's a surefire way to keep things cool, calm, and collected, all while ensuring that you're serving up a generous helping of positivity and growth. Who knew that managing self-talk could be as easy as making a sandwich? Just remember: the next time you feel like you're getting grilled, you've got the tools to flip the script and transform that critique into a tasty opportunity for growth. And if your inner critic complains about the flavor, tell it to go make its own darn sandwich!

Pause & Ponder: Sandwich Assembly Line

1 Identify a Recent "Critique": Think of a recent situation where your inner critic was particularly loud or harsh (e.g., after a small mistake, a less-than-perfect outcome, or a moment of impatience).

2 Practice the Compliment Sandwich on Yourself:

- **Top Bread (Genuine Compliment):** What did you do well, or what positive effort did you make in that situation? Be specific.

- **The Meat (Constructive Criticism):** What specific action or approach could you adjust or learn from next time? (Focus on the *action*, not on judging yourself.)

- **Bottom Bread (Reinforcing Compliment):** What's another positive quality or effort you demonstrated, or what positive outcome can you still find?

3 Say it out loud: How does it feel to "serve" this sandwich to yourself? Does it make the critique feel less overwhelming?

The Humorous Side of Self-Talk

Laughing at Yourself: The Best Medicine (No Prescription Needed – Unless You Have a Serious Case of Perpetual Seriousness)

In the bustling world of business, where deadlines loom larger than a sumo wrestler in a phone booth and meetings drag on longer than a Monday morning, it's easy to take ourselves too seriously. We don our professional masks, ready to conquer the day, but sometimes, we forget the most important tool in our arsenal: the ability to laugh at ourselves. Imagine walking into a meeting, tripping over your own feet (or, in my case, confidently walking into a glass door I was *sure* was open), and instead of cringing in embarrassment, you burst out laughing. That's the kind of resilience that keeps you cool under pressure. Plus, it's a lot more fun than sulking in a corner and plotting your revenge against gravity or inanimate objects.

Humor is a powerful antidote to stress, and when you can poke fun at your own blunders, you instantly lighten the atmosphere. It's like a cosmic "undo" button for awkwardness. Picture this: you accidentally send a cat meme to your entire team instead of the quarterly report. (Yes, it happens. Maybe not to *me*, but to a *friend*... who totally wasn't me.) Instead of hiding under your desk and letting your inner critic scream about career suicide, you turn it into a team-building exercise. "Clearly, my true calling lies in feline photography!" you announce, and suddenly, everyone is sharing their own ridiculous mishaps. You've transformed a potential disaster into a bonding moment, and just like that, your leadership skills shine brighter than your last PowerPoint presentation. You've gone from "clumsy professional" to "hilarious human who makes us feel better about *our* mistakes."

Let's face it, everyone has embarrassing moments; it's a part of being human. Whether it's forgetting a client's name right after they've introduced themselves (cue internal panic from my impatient brain: "Just remember it! Why can't you remember it?!") or mispronouncing a colleague's name for the hundredth time, the key is how you handle it. When you laugh at your own mistakes, you not only diffuse tension but also encourage others to do the same. It's like creating a safety net of humor in the workplace, where everyone feels free to share their slip-ups without fear of judgment. This camaraderie fosters a positive environment that can lead to increased collaboration and creativity—who knew that a little laughter could be so productive?

The Science Behind the Chuckle: Why Self-Deprecating Humor Works (When Done Right)

There's a real psychological benefit to laughing at yourself. It's not about putting yourself down in a truly damaging way, but rather about:

• **Reducing Perfectionism:** It reminds you that perfection is an illusion. When you embrace your flaws humorously, you reduce the pressure to be flawless, which is incredibly liberating.

• **Increasing Relatability:** People warm to authenticity. When you can laugh at your own foibles, others feel more comfortable with their own imperfections, fostering connection.

• **Boosting Resilience:** Humor acts as a buffer. It allows you to process negative experiences, extract the lesson, and then move on without getting stuck in self-pity. Each "blunder" becomes a humorous anecdote, a valuable part of your personal narrative.

• **Releasing Stress Hormones:** As mentioned before, laughter literally changes your brain chemistry. It reduces cortisol (the stress hormone) and releases endorphins, making you feel better, sharper, and more capable of handling what comes next.

Embracing humor in your professional life also helps cultivate a mindset of resilience. When you stop taking yourself too seriously, you open the door to learning from your mistakes instead of wallowing in self-pity. Think of each blunder as an opportunity for growth, wrapped in a hilarious package. When you can chuckle at your errors, you're reinforcing the idea that failure isn't the end of the world; it's just a plot twist in your story. And let's be honest, every good story needs a few laughs along the way, right? My own journey with impatience has given me a treasure trove of "plot twists," from sending emails to the wrong 'Reply All' group (oh, the humanity!) to blurting out half-formed ideas. Now, instead of dwelling, I try to find the absurd humor in it.

So, the next time you find yourself caught in a whirlwind of stress, or perhaps just tripped over your own enthusiasm, remember: laughter is the best medicine, and the prescription is as easy as a quick self-deprecating joke. Whether you're a high-powered executive or an everyday person navigating the trials of life, don't underestimate the power of humor. Laughing at yourself not only makes you more relatable but also turns those pressure-cooker moments into opportunities for connection and growth. So go ahead, trip on that conference room rug—just make sure to laugh about it afterward! And if you don't, I'll be here, laughing with you (not *at* you, mostly).

Pause & Ponder: Your Personal Blooper Reel

1 Recall a Recent "Blunder": Think of a recent embarrassing moment, mistake, or instance where your impatience (or other quirk) got the better of you.

2 Find the Humor: Can you find anything funny about it? What's the most absurd part? What would a comedian say about it?

3 The Humorous Reframe: Try to rephrase the incident in a lighthearted, self-deprecating way.

◦ *Example:* "I didn't forget my boss's name; I was merely giving him the unique experience of being momentarily nameless, a truly avant-garde approach to respect!"

◦ *My own impatient moment:* "I didn't interrupt; I was just enthusiastically pre-empting the next thought, which is basically a superpower when you're in a hurry... and sometimes a social faux pas."

4 Share (If You Dare!): If appropriate, consider sharing this humorous take with a trusted friend or colleague. Notice how it might diffuse your own stress and connect you with others.

Using Humor to Diffuse Tension: A Stand-Up Comedy Approach (No Stage Fright Required, Just a Good Punchline)

Using humor to diffuse tension can be as effective as a well-placed ice pack on a sprained ego. Imagine walking into a room full of stressed-out colleagues, each one more serious than a cat at a dog show. Instead of diving into the usual dreary discussions about quarterly earnings or project deadlines, why not break the ice with a joke? Or, even better, a relatable, lighthearted observation? Humor is like a secret weapon; it can transform a tense atmosphere into a lighthearted exchange faster than you can say, "Did you hear the one about the accountant who couldn't count?"

Consider a time when everything felt like it was spiraling out of control. Maybe a client was breathing down your neck, or a team member was on the verge of a meltdown over a presentation. My own impatient nature used to make me want to *scream* when things got tense and slow. But instead of succumbing to the weight of the moment, a well-timed quip can remind everyone that they're human. Picture a tense meeting where someone says, "This is going to be more complicated than explaining a selfie to my grandmother." The laughter that follows can reset everyone's mindset, making the challenges seem less daunting and the solutions more accessible. It's like someone just pressed the "reboot" button on the collective mood.

Of course, not all humor is created equal. The key is to keep it light, relatable, and *never* at someone else's expense (unless that "someone" is your own wonderfully imperfect self). Avoid jokes that could backfire like a poorly designed fireworks show. Political jokes? Best left for the family reunion, and even then, tread lightly. Instead, focus on the absurdities of everyday life, shared experiences, or gentle self-deprecation.

Types of Humor to Deploy When Tension Mounts:

1 Relatable Observation Humor: This is often the safest and most effective. You point out a shared experience that everyone can nod along to.

◦ *Example:* If everyone is scrambling before a deadline, you could say, "My brain feels like it's running on pure caffeine and a prayer right now. Anyone else feeling like they need a personal assistant just to find their coffee cup?"

◦ *My version, when my impatience flares:* "Is it just me, or does this meeting have more plot twists than a Netflix series, and I'm still waiting for the big reveal?!" (Said with a grin, of course).

2 Self-Deprecating Humor (The "I'm Human Too!" Card): This is fantastic for building rapport and showing vulnerability. It signals that you don't take yourself *too* seriously.

◦ *Example:* If you make a small error, "Well, I guess my brain decided to take a short vacation at that moment. My apologies, it usually sends a postcard."

◦ *My version, after blurting something out:* "My filter sometimes takes a coffee break without telling me. What I *meant* to convey was X, and I apologize if it came out like a hurried telegram!"

3 Absurdist/Lighthearted Analogies: Comparing a stressful situation to something silly or unexpected.

◦ *Example:* If a project is taking longer than expected, you might say, "I'm starting to think this project has more plot twists than a soap opera, and I'm not sure if I'm the hero or the villain yet!"

◦ *My version, when technology frustrates me:* "This software is more temperamental than my cat on bath day. We'll get there, eventually, probably after offering it some tuna."

Using humor effectively also means reading the room. There's a fine line between making people laugh and making them cringe. Gauge the mood and adapt your comedic timing accordingly. Sometimes a well-placed pun can lighten the mood, while at other times, a self-deprecating remark can show vulnerability and foster connection. "I've made more mistakes than a toddler with a crayon," can elicit giggles and create a sense of shared humanity, allowing people to breathe a little easier.

Incorporating humor into your self-talk can also be a game changer. When you find yourself spiraling into negativity before a big meeting, try flipping the script with a funny inner monologue. Instead of thinking, "I'm going to mess this up," switch to, "If I trip over my words, at least I'll give everyone a good story to tell, and maybe they'll think I'm just embracing my quirky side!" This shift in perspective not only boosts your confidence but also reminds you that laughter can be the best antidote to pressure. So next time you feel the tension rising, channel your inner stand-up comic and remember: a well-timed laugh (or even a well-timed internal chuckle) can turn a stressful situation into a memorable one. And who knows, you might even get a few new fans!

Pause & Ponder: Your Inner Stand-Up Routine

1 Recall a Tense Situation: Think of a recent situation where you or others felt tense, frustrated, or stressed.

2 Brainstorm Humorous Quips:

◦ Could you have used a relatable observation? (e.g., about the common struggle, the shared feeling of being overwhelmed).

◦ Could you have used self-deprecating humor? (e.g., a funny comment about your own momentary struggle or error).

◦ Could you have used a lighthearted analogy? (e.g., comparing the situation to something silly).

◦ *My Impatience Example:* If I'm feeling that impatient urge to speed things up, I might internally quip, "My internal clock is running on cheetah speed, while the world is operating on sloth time. Gotta adjust my settings!"

3 Practice (Low Stakes): The next time a minor moment of tension arises (e.g., someone is slow at the coffee machine, a brief tech glitch), try a small, internal humorous thought or, if appropriate, a very light, external quip. Notice how it might diffuse your own stress and connect you with others.

Self-Talk Strategies for Everyday Situations

The Elevator Pitch: Talking Yourself Up in 30 Seconds (Or, How to Avoid Being the Awkward Silence Person)

Picture this: you're in an elevator, the doors close, and suddenly you're trapped with the CEO of your dream company. Or, perhaps, a potential client, a fascinating industry contact, or even just someone who asks, "So, what do you do?" You have exactly 30 seconds (give or take a few floors) to make an impression before they hit the button for their floor and float away into the corporate stratosphere. No pressure, right? My own impatient brain in these situations is usually screaming, "Quick! Say something brilliant! Don't screw this up! Why is this elevator so slow?!"

This is where the elevator pitch swoops in like a superhero in a business suit. This micro-monologue is not just about selling yourself; it's about showcasing your personality, skills, and, let's face it, your ability to say something other than "Hi, I'm awkward" while staring intently at the floor numbers. The goal is to be memorable, intriguing, and leave them wanting more, all before the doors open again.

First, let's talk about the essentials of the elevator pitch. It's a mini commercial about you, but with a twist of charm and a sprinkle of wit. Your goal is to hit the sweet spot between informative and entertaining, like a well-crafted joke that actually has a punchline.

Key Components of a Killer (and Humorous) Elevator Pitch:

1 The Hook (Grab Their Attention!): You need something catchy that makes your listener perk up. Don't just start with your name and title.

○ *Instead of:* "Hi, I'm Jane and I'm a marketing manager."

○ *Try:* "Hi, I'm the person who can save your company from drowning in spreadsheets and turn them into dazzling success stories!"

○ My version: "Hi, I'm [Your Name], and I specialize in turning chaotic situations into surprisingly functional (and sometimes hilarious) solutions."

The more you can make them smile or raise an eyebrow in curiosity, the more likely they are to listen to the rest.

2 The Problem/Solution (What You Do, Simply): Clearly state what you do and, more importantly, what problem you help people or companies solve. Keep it concise; in the world of elevator pitches, brevity is your best friend.

○ *Example:* "Many businesses struggle with connecting with their audience online, so I craft engaging digital strategies that make their message irresistible."

○ *Adding humor:* "I'm a project manager who can juggle deadlines better than a circus performer with a caffeine addiction, ensuring your projects don't spontaneously combust."

3 The Benefit/Impact (Why Should They Care?): What's the positive outcome of what you do? This is where you connect your skills to their potential needs.

○ *Example:* "...This means they see real growth, happier customers, and less time spent pulling their hair out."

○ *With a dash of personality:* "Basically, I help clients sleep better at night, knowing their online presence is rocking. And who doesn't want more sleep?"

4 The Call to Action (What's Next?): Don't just stop cold. What do you want to happen next? Make it easy and, again, if possible, intriguing.

◦ *Instead of the usual:* "Let's connect."

◦ *Try:* "If you're looking for someone to turn chaos into clarity and perhaps infuse a little fun into the process, I might just be your superhero!"

◦ My version: "I'd love to chat more about how we might streamline things – I'm always looking for ways to make processes more efficient, ideally without anyone needing emergency coffee."

This leaves the door open for further conversation while maintaining that engaging tone. You want them to feel like they've just met someone interesting, not just another business card on a pile of monotony.

Self-Talk for Elevator Pitch Success:

Before you even step into that elevator (or open that networking event app), your self-talk is crucial. My old self would be panicking, replaying every past verbal stumble. The "cool under pressure" me uses these internal affirmations:

• "I am ready. I am articulate. I have something valuable to share."

• "My unique perspective is interesting, and people will enjoy my energy."

• "Even if I stumble, I'll recover with grace (and maybe a quick, self-deprecating chuckle)."

• "This is an opportunity to connect, not a test to pass perfectly."

Finally, practice until it flows like butter on warm toast. You want to deliver your pitch with confidence, not like you're reading a script written by a nervous squirrel. The more you practice, the more natural it will feel, even if you're rehearsing in front of your houseplants. And who knows? You might just find yourself in an elevator with that dream client or boss, ready to leave them thinking, "I need to know more about this delightful human!" Now go forth, and conquer those elevators—your future self (and their caffeine levels) will thank you!

Pause & Ponder: Your Personal Elevator Pitch Generator

1 Who are you? What's your core skill or passion? (e.g., problem-solver, creative thinker, efficiency expert, team builder, chaos coordinator).

2 What problem do you solve? (e.g., help companies connect with customers, streamline operations, inspire teams, calm anxious clients).

3 What's the unique "you" factor? What's your personality spice? (e.g., humor, calm demeanor, infectious enthusiasm, nononsense approach).

4 Draft your pitch: Combine these elements into a 30-second summary, focusing on a compelling hook and a clear call to action.

◦ *Example Starter:* "I'm the person who [Your Core Skill/Passion] so that [Problem You Solve] with a [Your Unique Factor] approach."

5 Inject some humor: How can you make it less formal and more memorable? A funny analogy, a relatable observation, or a quick self-deprecating quip.

6 Practice, practice, practice: Say it out loud. Record yourself. Refine it until it feels smooth, confident, and authentically *you*. And don't forget to smile!

Boardroom Battles: Staying Cool When Things Get Heated (And Avoiding the Urge to Throw Your Stapler)

In the high-stakes arena of boardroom battles, where egos clash louder than a toddler tantrum in a toy store, staying cool can feel like trying to ice skate on a flaming volcano. Picture this: you walk into a meeting armed with your best ideas, only to find your colleagues wielding their opinions like swords. They're ready to joust, and suddenly, your calm demeanor feels as out of place as a cat at a dog show. For someone like me, who often feels that surge of impatience when discussions go off-track or get overly aggressive, the initial impulse is to either retreat or, worse, jump into the fray with a sharp retort that I'll immediately regret.

But fear not, my friend! With the right self-talk and a few strategic maneuvers, you can turn that volcano into a spa day, or at least a slightly less scorching hot tub. It's about maintaining your composure even when the air crackles with tension, protecting your peace of mind, and ensuring your message is heard, not drowned out by the din.

First, let's talk about the art of **deep breathing**. Yes, it sounds like something out of a yoga retreat, but trust me, nothing says "I'm in control" quite like inhaling deeply while your heart races like a hamster on a wheel. When the tension in the room spikes, take a moment to breathe in as if you're about to savor the world's finest chocolate (or, in my case, that perfectly brewed coffee). Then exhale slowly, releasing not just your breath, but also that urge to throw your stapler at the person who just suggested your idea is as useful as a chocolate teapot. Repeat after me (internally, of course): "I am calm, I am collected, and I am definitely not throwing office supplies today." This physical act of conscious breathing actively shifts your nervous system away from panic.

Next up: the power of **positive affirmations**. Just like a superhero dons a cape, you too can don a mental shield against negativity. When someone starts hurling criticisms that feel more like personal attacks, channel your inner cheerleader. Instead of thinking, "Why is this person so rude? My idea is clearly brilliant! What is wrong with them?!" try, "This is an opportunity to showcase my brilliance and composure!" Or, if your impatience is flaring: "I am choosing to listen actively, not react impulsively. My value isn't tied to instant agreement." It's like turning a frown upside down, except you're flipping it into a dazzling smile that says, "You can't rattle me, my friend." Remember, even in the heat of battle, a little humor can disarm the most intense opponent. A well-timed, *appropriate* joke can diffuse tension faster than a microwave can pop popcorn.

Then there's the classic technique of **visualization**. Imagine your boardroom as a serene beach—complete with palm trees, gentle waves, and an endless supply of coconut water. When the discussions heat up, mentally transport yourself to this tropical paradise. Picture yourself in a hammock, gently swaying, while the chaos of the meeting fades into the background. You might even find yourself chuckling at the absurdity of it all. "Why are we arguing about quarterly projections when I could be sipping piña coladas?" This playful mental escapade will not only help keep you cool; it'll also make you the most relaxed person in the room (at least internally!).

Beyond the Mental: Active Listening and De-escalation

While your internal game is strong, remember that staying cool in a boardroom battle also involves how you interact externally.

• **Active Listening:** This is a superpower. When someone is aggressively challenging you, truly *listen* to understand their point, rather than just waiting for your turn to speak. Ask clarifying questions ("If I understand correctly, your concern is X?"). This not only gives you time to compose yourself but also often disarms the other person, as they feel heard.

• **Acknowledge and Reframe:** Instead of immediately defending, you can acknowledge their point before steering the conversation. "I hear your concern about the budget impact, and I appreciate you raising it. My proposal actually addresses that by..." This acknowledges their emotion without validating a personal attack.

• **Find Common Ground:** Look for shared objectives. "We all want this project to succeed, right?" This helps pivot from conflict to collaboration, even if you disagree on the *how*.

Finally, embrace the art of laughter. Nothing breaks the tension like a good chuckle, especially when someone accidentally reads the wrong slide or mispronounces a key term. Use these moments to lighten the mood. A well-placed quip can turn a fierce debate into a friendly discussion faster than you can say "Teamwork makes the dream work." The goal is to remind everyone that at the end of the day, we're all just humans trying to navigate this wild ride of business. So, when the boardroom feels more like a battlefield, just remember: stay cool, keep your self-talk upbeat, and don't forget to laugh your way through the chaos. The victory will taste all the sweeter!

Pause & Ponder: Your Boardroom Battle Plan

1 Identify a Common Trigger: What's one thing that often makes you lose your cool in a meeting or tense discussion? (e.g., interruptions, dismissive comments, endless tangents, slow decision-making).

2 Pre-Plan Your Self-Talk: Before your next potentially heated meeting, draft a few specific self-talk statements you can use *when* that trigger arises.

◦ *For interruptions:* "I am calm and will assert my point respectfully after they're finished."

◦ *For impatience:* "This is an opportunity to practice mindful listening. Slow down, breathe."

◦ *For dismissive comments:* "Their opinion doesn't define my worth or the value of my idea."

3 Choose a Composure Tool: Select one breathing technique or visualization to try the next time tension rises. Practice it for just 30 seconds.

4 Consider a Humorous Response (Internal or External): Can you think of a light, relatable, or self-deprecating quip you could use if appropriate? Even if you don't say it aloud, the internal chuckle can help.

Building a Personal Self-Talk Toolkit

Tools of the Trade: What You Need to Succeed (Because Even Superheroes Need a Utility Belt)

When it comes to navigating the wild world of business and life, having the right tools is as essential as knowing the difference between a stapler and a paperclip. You wouldn't head into a big meeting armed with a rusty old butter knife, right? (Unless you're trying a very niche, avant-garde approach to negotiation, which I don't recommend.) So let's equip you with the ultimate arsenal of self-talk tools that will keep you calm, cool, and collected, even when your boss starts using phrases like "synergy" and "circle back" with alarming frequency. Think of this as your personal utility belt, ready for any mental challenge.

First on the list is the trusty **positive affirmation**. Think of these little nuggets of encouragement as your personal cheerleader, minus the pom-poms and questionable dance moves. They're quick mental boosters that reframe your perspective. You could start your day with a simple mantra like, "I am a powerhouse of productivity, even before my first coffee," or "I handle stress like a pro, and I do it with a smile (mostly)." Just make sure you say it in front of a mirror — you'll look a little ridiculous, but hey, it's all part of the charm. And if you happen to encounter a tough client or a surprise meeting (the bane of my impatient existence), just repeat your affirmation like a mantra, and watch as your confidence grows faster than your coffee consumption.

Next, let's talk about **visualization**. Picture this: you're giving a presentation, and instead of imagining the audience in their underwear (which is a classic but often ineffective technique, trust me), visualize yourself as a confident, charismatic leader. You know, the type who makes even the most boring spreadsheet seem like a thrilling Netflix series. Close your eyes and see every detail — the applause, the nods, the free snacks afterward. The more vivid the imagery, the better the outcome. After all, if you can't picture success, how can you expect to achieve it? Your brain actually practices the desired outcome when you visualize, making it more likely to happen in reality.

Then there's the art of **deep breathing** — yes, the age-old trick that's far more effective than yelling into a pillow (though I've been known to try that in moments of extreme frustration, mostly due to slow Wi-Fi). When the pressure builds, and you feel like you're about to transform into the Hulk (or at least a very grumpy squirrel), take a moment to inhale deeply through your nose, hold it for a second, and exhale slowly through your mouth. It's like giving your brain a little spa day. And while you're at it, don't forget to throw in some silly affirmations while you breathe. "I am calm, I am cool, and I definitely do not resemble Godzilla right now." Just be careful where you practice this; the last thing you need is to scare your colleagues with your newfound Zen.

Finally, let's not ignore the power of **humor**. Laughter is the best medicine, especially when the stakes are high. So when you find yourself tangled in a web of deadlines and expectations, throw in a joke or two, even if it's just for your internal audience. "Why did the scarecrow win an award? Because he was outstanding in his field!" Use humor as a tool to lighten the mood, both for yourself and those around you. It's hard to stay stressed when you're chuckling over corny jokes, and it's a great way to bond with coworkers. It's my go-to for when my natural impatience threatens to spill over into a slightly sarcastic remark – a quick internal chuckle helps me choose a more constructive (and less regretful) response.

A New Tool for Your Belt: The Power of Mindfulness (It's Not Just for Monks Anymore)

You've got your affirmations, visualizations, breathing, and humor. Now, let's add another incredibly powerful tool to your arsenal: **mindfulness**. Don't worry, you don't need to sit cross-legged on a mountaintop, chanting. Mindfulness is simply the practice of being fully present in the moment, noticing your thoughts, feelings, and sensations *without judgment.*

Think of your mind as a bustling highway. Thoughts are the cars zipping by. Usually, we jump into one of those cars and get swept away by it – especially the loud, fast, impatient ones. Mindfulness teaches you to stand on the side of the highway, noticing the cars as they pass, but choosing not to get into any of them.

• **How it helps you stay cool:** When impatience flares, or stress builds, mindfulness allows you to *notice* the feeling ("Ah, there's that familiar tightening in my chest, that urge to rush"), rather than immediately *reacting* to it. This creates a tiny, but crucial, pause. In that pause, you can then deploy your breathing techniques, your affirmations, or your humor. It's the ultimate "spot check" for your internal state.

• **A quick exercise:** Next time you're drinking coffee (or tea, or water), don't just gulp it down. Take a moment. Notice the warmth of the mug, the aroma, the taste on your tongue. Just for 30 seconds. That's mindfulness. It's about bringing awareness to the everyday.

So grab these tools, get ready to wield them like a pro, and watch as you become the calmest, coolest, and most collected version of yourself, even when the pressure is on! Remember, this isn't about being perfect; it's about having a rich, varied toolkit that you can playfully pull from when life throws you a curveball (or, in my case, a particularly slow-moving queue).

Pause & Ponder: Building Your Personal Toolkit

1 Toolkit Audit: From all the tools we've discussed (Affirmations, Visualization, Deep Breathing, Humor, Mindfulness), which 2-3 resonate most with you right now?

2 Immediate Application: Pick one tool you'd like to actively try to use more this week.

- *Example:* "I will try Box Breathing for 1 minute before my morning team meeting."

- *My personal example:* "I will try to be mindful of my impatience in traffic, noticing the feeling without letting it completely derail me, and then perhaps try a humorous reframe."

3 Combine Forces: How might you combine two tools? (e.g., using a humorous affirmation while practicing deep breathing, or visualizing success with a mindful focus).

Crafting Your Daily Mantra: Make It Catchy! (Your Brain's New Favorite Jingle)

Crafting a daily mantra is like choosing the perfect outfit for a big meeting; it needs to be catchy, comfortable, and just the right amount of eye-catching. You wouldn't want to stroll into a boardroom wearing something that screams "I just rolled out of bed" (unless that's your signature power move, in which case, own it!). Similarly, your mantra should be snappy enough to grab your attention and remind you that you're a force to be reckoned with. Start brainstorming by thinking about what makes you feel like a rock star, even on days when the coffee hasn't kicked in yet.

Now, let's spice things up a bit. Instead of the usual "I can do this" or "I am strong," why not jazz it up with a little humor? How about "I'm so calm, even my coffee is jealous"? This kind of playful twist not only makes your mantra memorable but also makes you chuckle every time you say it. Laughter is a fantastic stress buster, and if your mantra can evoke a giggle, then you're halfway to feeling cool under pressure. For my own impatient tendencies, I might try: "My calm is so profound, even snails ask me for meditation tips," or "I embody the graceful patience of a sloth... on a particularly zen day."

Remember, your mantra should resonate with you in a way that feels authentic. If you're a numbers person, try something like "I'm as steady as a well-calibrated spreadsheet, even when the data throws a tantrum." If you're more of a creative type, perhaps "I'm the Picasso of problem-solving, turning challenges into colorful masterpieces" might do the trick. The key is to make sure it reflects your personality while also packing a punch. After all, if you can't take yourself lightly, how can you expect others to, especially during tense moments at work?

Once you've settled on a few contenders, it's time to put them to the test. Say them out loud and see how they feel in your mouth. If they make you feel like a million bucks, you're on the right track. If they sound more like a bad joke (and not the good, self-deprecating kind!), toss them aside and keep experimenting. This is *your* mantra; it should resonate with your inner superhero. And speaking of superheroes, if your mantra can make you feel like you can leap tall buildings in a single bound (or at least tackle that email avalanche without spilling your coffee), then you've hit the jackpot.

Finally, don't forget to sprinkle a little flair into your mantra routine. Write it on sticky notes and plaster them around your workspace, or create a funky phone background that reminds you of your mantra every time you check the time. You could even use it as your password hint (though maybe not the actual password!). The more you see and say it, the more it will become a part of your daily groove. In no time, you'll be strutting through your day with a mantra that's not just catchy but also keeps you cool, calm, and collected, no matter what curveballs come your way. Think of it as installing a permanent "happy thought" app directly into your brain.

Pause & Ponder: Your Mantra Mixer

1 Core Desire: What is one core quality or feeling you want to amplify in your daily life? (e.g., patience, resilience, focus, joy, confidence, groundedness).

2 Brainstorm Unique Hooks: Think of a personal metaphor, a funny image, or a relatable struggle that you can flip on its head with humor.

  ◦ *For patience:* Imagine the opposite of impatience – a sloth, a turtle, a perfectly brewed cup of tea.

  ◦ *For resilience:* A rubber band, a bounce house, a comeback kid.

3 Draft Your Catchy Mantra: Combine your core desire with your unique hook. Aim for something short, memorable, and authentically *you*.

 ◦ *Examples:*

  ■ "I am the unshakeable force, calm as a cucumber wearing sunglasses in a tornado."

  ■ "My mind is a serene lake, even when the ducks of distraction are doing a frantic dance."

  ■ "I embrace changes like a surprise party – a little startled at first, but ultimately ready for cake!"

4 The Smile Test: Say your mantra aloud. Does it make you smile, even just a little? If so, you've found a winner!

Overcoming Obstacles with Self-Talk

Facing Failure: Turning It into Your Best Friend (Even If It's a Slightly Annoying Friend Who Eats All Your Snacks)

Failure is like that unexpected guest at a party who shows up uninvited, eats all the snacks, and somehow manages to spill red wine on your new carpet. At first, you might want to kick them out, or at least lock yourself in the bathroom until they leave. My impatient side used to immediately jump to, "This is a disaster! Why couldn't I have just done it right the first time?! Now everything's ruined!" The immediate thought process is rarely, "Oh, how delightful, a learning opportunity!"

But here's the kicker: they might actually have some valuable life lessons tucked away under that embarrassing behavior. In the world of business and personal growth, failure is an unavoidable companion, and instead of treating it like an unwelcome pest, we should embrace it like a quirky friend—one who just happens to have a knack for teaching us the hard way. Think of it as life's way of giving you a "practice run" before the real show.

Think about it: every time you trip over a hurdle, you're given a fantastic opportunity to learn how to jump higher next time. Sure,

48

the first few attempts might leave you face-down in the mud, covered in metaphorical (or literal) dirt, but that's just part of the process. Each flop is merely a stepping stone toward success, and if you can dust yourself off and laugh at the absurdity of it all, you'll find that failure can be a surprisingly good sport. It's the comedic relief in your serious business drama, reminding you not to take life too seriously. After all, who doesn't love a good blooper reel? Even the most brilliant inventions (like sticky notes, or even penicillin!) were often "failures" that led to accidental triumphs.

Now, let's talk self-talk. When failure knocks on your door, it's easy to let negative thoughts take the mic and belt out a sad ballad. "I'm a failure." "I'll never get this right." "Why did I think I could do this? I'm clearly not cut out for it!" This is your "Overgeneralization" cognitive distortion working overtime, turning one stumble into a lifetime sentence. But hold on! Instead of letting those sad tunes play on repeat, how about you put on a new record? Imagine yourself saying, "Hey, failure, you sneaky little rascal, thanks for showing me what *doesn't* work! Now we know what to avoid on the next attempt." You'd be surprised how much lighter life feels when you change the tune from "woe is me" to "let's dance this out!"

If you want to turn failure into your best friend, practice the art of **positive affirmations** and **reframing**. These little nuggets of wisdom can turn even the grumpiest of failures into your biggest fan. Instead of wallowing in despair, try repeating to yourself, "Every misstep is a step toward mastery," or "I may have stumbled, but I'm also learning how to do the cha-cha (and probably avoiding a much bigger trip later!)." Or, my own go-to when my impatience causes a misstep: "Well, that was a hurried disaster. Next time, I'll channel the speed of a sloth and the wisdom of an owl before acting!" Soon enough, you'll find that failure isn't just a friend; it's your biggest cheerleader, waving pom-poms made of lessons learned and resilience gained.

Embracing the "Growth Mindset": Your Secret Weapon

A powerful concept that helps us befriend failure is the **growth mindset**, popularized by psychologist Carol Dweck.

• **Fixed Mindset:** Believes abilities are fixed. If you fail, it means you're not smart enough, talented enough, etc. ("I failed, therefore I *am* a failure.") This mindset avoids challenges and gives up easily.

• **Growth Mindset:** Believes abilities can be developed through dedication and hard work. Failure is seen as an opportunity to learn and improve. ("I failed, what can I learn from this? How can I do better next time?") This mindset embraces challenges and persists in the face of setbacks.

When your self-talk supports a growth mindset, failure isn't an indictment of your character; it's simply feedback. It's a signpost on the road, not the end of the journey. Humor helps immensely here, as it reduces the perceived threat of failure, allowing you to approach it with curiosity rather than dread.

Lastly, remember that even the most successful business moguls faced their fair share of failures. Steve Jobs was famously fired from Apple, the company he co-founded. Walt Disney's first animation studio went bankrupt. J.K. Rowling's *Harry Potter* manuscript was rejected by numerous publishers. Picture them in their early days, probably looking a bit like a deer caught in headlights, wondering how they ended up in such a mess. But they didn't let that stop them. Instead, they turned those moments into stories of triumph, with a sprinkle of humor to keep things light. So the next time failure comes knocking, invite it in for a cup of coffee, share a laugh, and learn how to turn those awkward moments into powerful stepping stones on your path to success. Because let's be honest, a perfectly smooth journey makes for a terribly boring story, and you, my friend, are crafting an epic!

Pause & Ponder: Your Failure Resume (with a Twist!)

Let's turn your "failures" into badges of honor.

1 List 1-2 Recent "Failures" or Setbacks: These can be big or small – a missed deadline, an awkward interaction, a project that didn't go as planned, a moment your impatience got the better of you.

2 What Did You Learn? For each, identify a concrete lesson. Even if it's "I learned I need more sleep," or "I learned that rushing actually makes things slower."

3 The Humorous Reframe: Now, rewrite each "failure" as a humorous growth experience, focusing on the lesson learned.

◦ *Original:* "I totally messed up that presentation pitch."

◦ *Reframed:* "My presentation pitch was a masterclass in 'what not to do,' providing invaluable data on how to perfectly pivot for next time. I'm now a certified pitch-ologist!"

◦ *My personal reframing of an impatient outburst:* "My internal 'hurry up' alarm went off so loud I accidentally shared my urgency with everyone. Lesson learned: internal alarms need internal mute buttons, and a more patient re-entry strategy!"

4 Embrace It: How does it feel to see your "failures" not as endings, but as stepping stones with a side of comedy?

The Fear Factor: Talking Yourself Off the Ledge (Before Your Brain Convinces You to Build a Fort Under Your Desk)

The fear factor is a sneaky little gremlin that often shows up right when you're about to take a leap of faith. Picture this: you're about to pitch a brilliant idea to your boss, and suddenly, your brain decides it's the perfect time to play a greatest hits album of all your past failures. "Remember that time you accidentally sent the wrong presentation to the client? Good times! Or that time you completely froze when asked a direct question? Ah, memories!" This is where self-talk comes in. Instead of letting fear take the wheel and drive you straight into a fort made of throw pillows under your desk, it's time to channel your inner motivational speaker and talk yourself off that ledge like a pro.

First things first, let's acknowledge that fear is as common as coffee breaks in the office. Everyone experiences it, from the CEO contemplating a risky merger to the intern who just realized they've been spelling "synergy" wrong all week. (Side note: "synergy" is often a fear-inducing word in itself, so maybe we should just avoid it.) The trick is to recognize fear for what it is: a distraction, a loud, sometimes theatrical, warning system that often overreacts. You wouldn't let a tiny spider ruin your entire day, right? So why let a little fear derail your ambitions? When fear creeps in, grab your metaphorical megaphone and remind yourself of all the times you've triumphed. "Hey, remember that presentation you nailed? And how you handled that awkward client call like a seasoned pro? Yeah, you're kind of a big deal!"

Understanding Your Fear (and Its Funny Manifestations):

Fear isn't just a mental state; it's a full-body experience, often with hilarious (in retrospect) physical manifestations. Your self-talk can help you decode and manage these.

• **The "Sweaty Palms & Racing Heart" Gala:** This is your body's "fight or flight" response kicking in. Your self-talk can reframe it: "Ah, that's just my body getting pumped up and ready for action, like a super-energetic fan at a rock concert!"

• **The "Brain Freeze" Moment:** You know, when your mind goes blank? "My brain is just doing a quick system reboot. I'll take a breath, and the answers will flow back in like a perfectly timed download."

• **The "Internal Scream" (My Personal Favorite for Impatience):** When the urge to *rush* or *flee* is overwhelming. "Okay, Inner Cheetah, calm down. We're going for calm and collected, not a frantic sprint."

Next up, let's sprinkle some humor on that fear sandwich. When fear tries to convince you that you'll flop harder than a fish out of water, counter it with the absurdity of the situation. Picture yourself standing in front of your audience, and instead of imagining them judging you harshly, visualize them in ridiculous outfits. Suddenly, your boss is wearing a clown wig while your coworkers sport tutu skirts and mismatched socks. The laughter from this mental image can ease the tension and remind you that, in the grand scheme of things, it's just a presentation, not a life-or-death mission. Unless, of course, you're presenting to a jury of actual clowns, in which case, the tutu visualization might backfire.

Of course, positive affirmations are the bread and butter of self-talk. "I am capable, I am confident, and I definitely know how to work a PowerPoint (and fix it if it crashes)." Start your day with these affirmations, and watch how they transform your mindset. They're like the espresso shot your brain needs to kick-start the engine. When fear strikes, repeat those affirmations like a mantra. "I am not afraid of public speaking; I am merely auditioning for the role of 'Most Entertaining Presenter'!" Embracing humor and positivity in your self-talk makes fear feel less like an insurmountable mountain and more like a pesky molehill you can easily step over (or perhaps perform a dramatic leap over, just for show).

Beyond the Ledge: What to Do When Fear Persists

Sometimes, fear isn't just a fleeting thought; it's a deeply ingrained habit. If you find your self-talk constantly dragging you to the "ledge," consider these actions:

• **Small Steps Forward:** Don't try to conquer Mount Everest in one go. Break down the fearful situation into tiny, manageable steps. If public speaking scares you, start by speaking up for one minute in a small meeting. Then two. Celebrate each tiny win.

• **Seek Support:** You don't have to face your fears alone. Talk to friends, family, or a trusted coworker about your fears. You'll find that sharing these thoughts often leads to a hearty laugh and a sense of camaraderie. My own experience with sharing my impatience struggles has revealed that most people understand; they just appreciate the awareness! After all, nothing bonds people quite like laughing about the absurdity of their fears.

• **"What's the Worst That Can Happen?" (With a Punchline):** Sometimes, running through the absolute worst-case scenario can be oddly calming, especially when you add humor.

○ *Worst Case:* "I mess up the presentation, they fire me, I lose my house, I end up living in a van down by the river."

○ *Humorous Reframe:* "Well, at least I'll have a great story for my memoir, and I've always wanted to try van life. Plus, my cat would probably enjoy the river view." This isn't about being irresponsible, but about demonstrating that even the "worst" isn't as terrifying as your brain makes it out to be.

Finally, when the fear monster rears its ugly head, remember that you're not alone in this wild ride of life. Everyone has their moments of doubt—yes, even that colleague who seems to have it all figured out. So, the next time you feel like you're teetering on the edge, take a deep breath, summon your inner comedian, and talk yourself back to solid ground. You've got this! And if you still feel a little wobbly, just imagine me on the sidelines, cheering you on (and probably tripping over my own feet, just to remind you it's okay).

Pause & Ponder: Your Fear Face-Off

1 Identify a Specific Fear: What's one fear that holds you back or makes you lose your cool? (e.g., fear of rejection, public speaking, conflict, making a big mistake, looking foolish).

2 The "Worst Case" (with a Twist): Briefly imagine the *absolute worst* that could realistically happen if this fear came true. Now, how can you add a humorous, slightly absurd twist to that worst-case scenario?

○ *Example: Fear of public speaking:* "I'll trip, forget my lines, and accidentally project a photo of my cat in a sombrero. *Worst Case Twist:* At least everyone will leave remembering the sombrero cat, and I'll be famous on internal Slack channels."

3 Your "Ledge Talk": Craft 2-3 self-talk statements or affirmations you can use when this specific fear arises, incorporating humor or a "growth mindset" perspective.

○ *Example for fear of rejection:* "If they say no, it just means they're saving the 'yes' for something even more epic. My resilience is like a boomerang – it always comes back stronger!"

4 Small Step, Big Courage: What's one *tiny* action you can take this week to face that fear, even just a little? (e.g., speak up once in a meeting, ask a low-stakes question, send that slightly intimidating email).

Self-Talk in Relationships

~~~

Communicating with Confidence: Say What You Mean, Mean What You Say (And Avoid Accidental Bluntness)

Communicating with confidence is like walking a tightrope while juggling flaming torches—terrifying yet exhilarating. Imagine standing in front of an audience, your palms clammy, heart racing, and the only thing standing between you and a successful presentation is your ability to articulate thoughts that sound like they belong in a boardroom, not a sitcom. My own personal struggle here is often the inverse: my brain works so fast that my mouth can outpace my filter, leading to unintentional bluntness. I might think, "That's a bit slow," and it comes out sounding like, "Are you operating on dial-up?" (Again, apologies to anyone I've done that to.)

But fear not! Saying what you mean and meaning what you say doesn't require a PhD in Linguistics or a lifetime supply of throat lozenges. With a sprinkle of self-talk and a dash of humor, you can tackle this challenge head-on, ensuring your words build bridges, not burn them.

First off, let's address the elephant in the room: the fear of public speaking. It's so common that there should be a support group for it. You can picture it now—"Hello, my name is Bob, and I'm terrified of talking in front of people, especially after I accidentally called my boss 'Mom' last week." But here's the kicker: the trick to communicating with confidence is to embrace that fear, give it a name (maybe Gerald, or for me, "Captain Impatience"), and then tell Gerald to take a hike. When you start your sentences with "I am confident and clear," instead of "I hope I don't trip over my words and offend everyone," you'll find that the words flow smoother than a well-oiled machine. Think of it as upgrading your internal software from "nervous wreck" to "cool, calm, and collected communicator."

Next, let's delve into the art of clarity. It's vital to say what you mean, and the best way to do that is to ditch the jargon and corporate mumbo-jumbo. Nobody wants to hear you use phrases like "synergize our core competencies" when "let's work together" will do just fine. Keep it simple, keep it real, and your audience will be nodding along instead of wondering if you've just summoned a spell from a business wizard. Add a touch of humor to lighten the mood—maybe a quirky anecdote about how you once confused "ROI" with "really overripe iguanas." Trust me, people will remember your message long after they've stopped chuckling. For me, this means consciously slowing down my internal thought process just enough to pick the *kindest* and *clearest* words, rather than just the fastest.

Now, let's talk about **body language**. You might be saying all the right things, but if your arms are crossed tighter than a clam at high tide, your message isn't getting through. Stand tall, make eye contact (not a creepy stare, just a friendly gaze), and remember to smile—not like you're plotting something sinister, but like you just won the lottery (and maybe bought everyone a ticket!). When your body is open and inviting, your words will carry more weight. Besides, who doesn't want to look like they just walked off the set of a motivational speaker convention, complete with a dazzling smile and a flair for the dramatic? Your self-talk can remind you: "Shoulders back, smile on, radiating calm, not chaos."

Beyond Speaking: The Power of Listening (Yes, Even for the Impatient!)

Confident communication isn't just about what you say; it's profoundly about how well you *listen*. For someone who struggles with impatience, this is often the biggest hurdle. My brain is already five steps ahead, formulating my response before the other person has even finished their sentence. But truly listening is a superpower that builds rapport and earns respect.

• **Active Listening:** This means giving the speaker your full attention, nodding, making eye contact, and showing engagement. Your self-talk during listening could be: "Listen to understand, not to reply. Embrace the pause."

• **Empathy:** Try to understand the other person's perspective or feelings, even if you don't agree. "I understand why you might feel frustrated." This validates their experience and opens the door for a more productive conversation.

• **Don't Interrupt (Unless it's an Emergency!):** This is a tough one for the fast-thinking among us. Consciously bite your tongue. Tell your self-talk: "Wait for it... wait for it... their turn is almost done. My brilliant point will still be brilliant in 10 more seconds."

Lastly, practice makes perfect, but let's not pretend it's all sunshine and rainbows. You might feel like a fool rehearsing in front of your bathroom mirror, but trust me, that reflection is a judgment-free zone. Use affirmations to boost your confidence— try something like, "I am a master communicator, and I can charm the socks off a room full of CEOs (and maybe even impress my cat with my new vocal range)." The more you say it, the more you'll start to believe it. Eventually, you'll find yourself in a boardroom, confidently sharing your ideas while Gerald the Fear (or Captain Impatience) sits in the corner, sipping tea and contemplating his life choices. With each confident word, you'll be well on your way to becoming the calm, cool, collected communicator you've always wanted to be.

Pause & Ponder: Your Communication Confidence Boost

1 Identify a Communication Challenge: What's one type of conversation or situation where you struggle to communicate confidently, or where your impatience tends to get the better of you? (e.g., giving feedback, asking for a raise, disagreeing with a colleague, speaking to authority figures).

2 Pre-Game Self-Talk: Before that situation arises, craft 2-3 specific self-talk statements to boost your confidence and remind you to be calm and clear.

◦ *Example for disagreeing:* "I can express my opinion respectfully and clearly. My perspective is valuable."

◦ *My self-talk for avoiding accidental bluntness:* "Breathe. Think before speaking. Choose kindness over speed. My words have power."

3 Practice Active Listening: In your next conversation, make a conscious effort to truly *listen* without interrupting. Notice how this changes the dynamic and your own internal state.

4 Embrace Body Language: Pick one positive body language cue (e.g., eye contact, open posture, a genuine smile) to focus on during your next interaction.

The Power of "I" Statements: Not Just for Therapists (Also Great for Office Politics and Laundry Negotiations)

When you hear "I" statements, you might conjure images of therapists scribbling furiously in their notepads while you pour your heart out, perhaps recounting the time you spent an hour looking for your keys only to find them in the refrigerator. But let's face it, "I" statements aren't just for couch-sitting, tea-sipping professionals. They're for everyone who wants to keep their cool in the chaos of board meetings, family dinners, or even the occasional trip to the grocery store when someone steals the last avocado right out from under your nose. It's time to embrace the power of "I" statements, not just for mental health, but for everyday sanity!

So, what exactly is an "I" statement? Simply put, it's a way of expressing your feelings, thoughts, or needs by focusing on *your* experience, rather than placing blame or judgment on someone else. It typically follows a structure like: **"I feel [emotion] when [situation/behavior] because [reason/impact]."**

Imagine this: you're in a meeting, and your colleague just suggested the most ridiculous idea since someone thought it was a good idea to wear socks with sandals. Your immediate internal monologue, especially if you're like me and struggle with impatience, might be: "That's a terrible idea! What are they thinking? They're clearly clueless!" If you blurt out, "Your idea is ridiculous!" you're guaranteed to get a defensive reaction and probably start a boardroom battle.

Instead, you can use an "I" statement. Try saying, **"I feel concerned that this idea might not align with our current strategic goals, because I envision potential roadblocks in its implementation."** Suddenly, you sound like a composed professional, not a drama queen ready to throw a chair. Plus, you might just plant the seed of doubt in their mind without causing a scene, and who doesn't want to be the subtle genius in the room? This shifts the conversation from an attack to a shared problem-solving effort.

The beauty of "I" statements is that they also help you express feelings without sounding like you're about to unleash the Kraken. Instead of saying, "You never listen to my ideas!" which might elicit defensive reactions and make the other person shut down (and my impatient self used to be *very* guilty of this!), try, **"I feel overlooked when my ideas aren't discussed, because I believe they could contribute positively to the project."** This way, you express your feelings without pointing fingers, making it less likely that anyone will storm out of the room in a huff. And let's be honest, no one wants to be the person who causes a dramatic exit over a missed idea.

"I" Statements in Action: Beyond the Boardroom

The power of "I" statements extends far beyond the professional sphere. They can transform family dynamics, friendships, and even interactions with strangers.

- **At Home (Laundry Negotiations):**
  ◦ *Instead of:* "You always leave your dirty socks everywhere!" (Blaming, accusatory)
  ◦ *Try:* **"I feel frustrated when I see socks on the floor, because it makes the house feel messy to me."** (Expresses your feeling and the impact on *you*).
- **With a Friend (When Plans Change Last Minute):**
  ◦ *Instead of:* "You're always cancelling on me! You don't care about our plans." (Judgmental, assuming intent)
  ◦ *Try:* **"I feel disappointed when our plans change last minute, because I was really looking forward to our time together."** (Communicates your feeling without attacking their character).
- **In Public (When Someone Cuts in Line - for my impatient self!):**
  ◦ *Instead of:* (Muttering under breath) "Seriously? The nerve of some people! Just cut right in, why don't you?!" (Internal rage-building)
  ◦ *Try (if you dare, and with a calm tone!):* **"Excuse me, I believe I was next in line."** (A factual "I" statement, expressing your observation and expectation, rather than a heated accusation.) Even just the *internal* formation of this thought, choosing to be calm and clear, is powerful.

It's amazing how a simple shift in language can turn a potential battlefield into a peaceful negotiation zone, or at least a less emotionally charged one. Who knew that mastering communication could make you the ultimate family diplomat, or the calmest person in the grocery store?

Why They Work (and How They Help You Stay Cool):
- **Reduces Defensiveness:** When you start with "I feel," the

other person is less likely to feel attacked and more likely to listen to your perspective.

• **Clarity:** You clearly state *your* experience, making it easier for others to understand your needs.

• **Empowerment:** You take responsibility for your own feelings and reactions, rather than making them dependent on someone else's behavior. This gives you a sense of control and helps you stay calm.

• **Authenticity:** It allows you to express your genuine emotions in a constructive way, fostering deeper connections.

In the end, incorporating "I" statements into your everyday conversations is like adding a secret ingredient to your favorite recipe. Whether you're in the office, at home, or just trying to survive the wild world of social interactions, these statements can help you communicate clearly and effectively. So, the next time you feel the urge to unleash your inner drama llama (or, in my case, the impatient "let's just get this over with" ram), take a breath, use an "I" statement, and watch as you navigate the waters of life with newfound coolness and charm. You'll not only keep your cool but maybe even earn a few nods of respect along the way. And who knows, maybe that avocado thief will even apologize!

Pause & Ponder: Your "I" Statement Playbook

1 Recall a Challenging Interaction: Think of a recent situation where you felt frustrated, angry, or misunderstood by someone else.

2 Rewrite with Blame: Briefly write down how you might have *originally* expressed your feeling, likely starting with "You always..." or "You never..."

3 Transform with "I" Statements: Now, using the "I feel [emotion] when [situation/behavior] because [reason/impact]" structure, rewrite that interaction using "I" statements.

 ◦ *Original (internal thought for impatience):* "He's wasting my time with all these unnecessary details!"

 ◦ *Transformed:* "I feel anxious when the discussion goes into extensive detail, because I'm concerned about our looming deadline."

4 Practice in Low Stakes: Find an opportunity this week to use an "I" statement in a low-stakes situation (e.g., with a friend about a minor annoyance, or a colleague about a simple preference). Notice how it changes the interaction.

Putting It All Together

Daily Practices: Making Self-Talk a Habit (Because Your Brain Loves a Good Routine, Especially a Fun One)

The first step in making self-talk a habit is to recognize that your inner dialogue is like a quirky stand-up comedian with a penchant for self-deprecation. You wouldn't let a comedian bomb on stage every day, so why let your inner critic take center stage? Instead, it's time to give that voice a makeover. Treat it like a friend you're trying to cheer up after a rough day. Start by replacing negative comments with playful banter. "Oh, you forgot that presentation? No worries, just think of it as an impromptu performance art piece!" Or, my own inner monologue when my impatience tries to take over: "Alright, inner speed demon, let's try channeling that energy into something productive, like making coffee faster, not just thinking about it faster." With a little humor, you can transform self-talk from a dreaded monologue into a delightful dialogue.

Once you've established a basic rapport with your inner voice, it's time to schedule regular chat sessions. Yes, you heard that right. Just like you wouldn't skip a meeting with a potential client (unless you enjoy awkward silence), don't skip your daily self-talk. Set aside a few minutes each day, preferably while you're doing something mundane, like brushing your teeth, doing the dishes, or waiting for your coffee to brew. This is prime time for some uplifting affirmations. "I am a rockstar in the boardroom, even if my socks don't match," or "I handle crises like a duck handles water—gracefully and without a care (on the surface, at least!)" Soon, your bathroom mirror will feel like a motivational stage where the only audience is you, and that's just fine.

As you cultivate this habit, don't shy away from the ridiculousness of it all. Embrace the absurdity! Try talking to yourself in different accents or as if you were giving a TED Talk to your houseplants. "Ladies and gentlemen of the fern community, today we discuss the art of remaining calm under pressure, even when the Wi-Fi acts like a toddler throwing a tantrum!" The silliness of it can break the ice and make self-talk less of a chore and more of a joyful, albeit slightly absurd, ritual. Who knew that motivating yourself could come with a side of comedy? This playful approach helps your brain actually *enjoy* the process of adopting new habits.

Consistency is key, but remember that we're all human. There will be days when your self-talk sounds more like a grumpy cat than a motivational guru. On those days, it's essential to lighten up and not take yourself too seriously. Perhaps when your self-talk turns pessimistic, you could respond with, "Oh come on, inner critic! Give me a break; even the best comedians have off days! Let's get back on script, shall we?" This playful pushback not only acknowledges the negativity but also reminds you that it's okay to stumble in the process. It's a "progress, not perfection" mantra in action. For my impatient self, a bad day might mean a slip into bluntness. My self-talk now shifts to: "Well, that was a hurried delivery. Next time, I'll remember the slow-motion button. It's a learning curve, and I'm gracefully (mostly) navigating it."

Lastly, keep track of your progress and celebrate the little victories. Did you manage to talk yourself out of a meltdown during a stressful meeting? High five yourself! Did you remind yourself that you're capable of more than just surviving Monday? Treat yourself to a favorite snack! Keeping a journal of these moments can serve as both a reminder of how far you've come and a source of amusement when you look back. After all, who wouldn't want to read about the time you successfully convinced yourself that forgetting the coffee order was a sign of your artistic genius for spontaneous adaptation? Making self-talk a habit doesn't have to be all serious business; a little laughter can go a long way in keeping you cool under pressure.

Pause & Ponder: Your Daily Self-Talk Schedule

Let's design a simple "self-talk schedule" for your week.

1 Morning Ritual (5 minutes): How will you start your day with empowering self-talk? (e.g., a specific affirmation in the mirror, mindful breathing before checking emails, a quick humorous reframe of upcoming tasks).

  ° *My morning ritual:* Acknowledge any morning impatience, then immediately affirm: "I choose calm and clarity today, even if my brain wants to race."

2 Mid-Day Check-in (1-2 minutes): When will you pause and check in with your inner voice? (e.g., during a coffee break, before lunch, after a challenging meeting). What tool will you use? (e.g., Box Breathing, a quick Compliment Sandwich for yourself, a humorous observation).

3 Evening Reflection (5 minutes): Before bed, how will you review your day's self-talk? (e.g., recall one "win" you celebrated, acknowledge a "learning moment" with humor, practice gratitude).

4 "On the Fly" Trigger Practice: Identify one specific trigger (e.g., slow tech, a long line, unexpected changes). When it happens, practice using a chosen self-talk tool (affirmation, breathing, reframe).

Celebrating Your Wins: Because You Deserve It! (And Because Your Brain Needs a High-Five)

Celebrating your wins is like throwing a surprise party for

yourself, and let's be honest, who doesn't love a good party? Whether you closed that tricky deal, finally tackled your never-ending to-do list, or simply survived another Monday without succumbing to the urge to debate the existential meaning of spreadsheets, it's time to pop the confetti and bust out the imaginary champagne. The beauty of celebrating your wins lies in the fact that it doesn't have to be extravagant. A simple "You did it!" while doing a little happy dance in your office (doors closed, perhaps, unless you want to inspire an impromptu office rave) will do just fine. Remember, you are the star of your own show, and if the audience (a.k.a. you) doesn't applaud, who will?

Now, you might be thinking, "But my wins are so small! I just got through a particularly slow queue at the grocery store without grumbling." Ah, the classic case of the humble pie. Let's set the record straight: small wins are still wins! Did you manage to show up to that meeting on time despite a last-minute traffic jam? Win! Did you resist the urge to eat that third donut at the office, even though it was calling your name? Win! Did you remember to water your office plant, which has miraculously survived your black thumb for another week? Triple win! Celebrating these little victories is like adding sprinkles to your ice cream; they might seem insignificant, but they make the experience so much sweeter. And let's be real, who doesn't want their life to be a little sweeter? These small celebrations create tiny bursts of dopamine, reinforcing the positive behaviors and making you more likely to repeat them. It's science, disguised as a party!

In the business world, we often get so caught up in the next big goal that we forget to kick back and acknowledge the milestones we've already crossed. It's like running a marathon and never bothering to stop and take a selfie at the finish line. Allowing yourself to celebrate these achievements, no matter how minor, not only boosts your confidence but also acts as a powerful motivator. Next time you close a deal, treat yourself to a fancy coffee or take a moment to do a victory lap around the office. Trust us, your colleagues will either join in or think you've finally lost it, but either way, you'll be the one winning! For my own impatient self, successfully navigating a slow process without a single sigh or eye-roll is a monumental victory, worthy of at least a mental ticker-tape parade.

Let's talk about the art of **self-talk** during these celebratory moments. If you find yourself downplaying your achievements with a dismissive wave of the hand ("Oh, it was nothing"), it's time to upgrade your internal dialogue. Instead of saying, "It was just a fluke, anyone could have done that," try, "I am a genius, and everyone should bow down to my brilliance (but subtly, of course, because modesty)." Okay, maybe not *that* dramatic, but you get the point. Positive affirmations can transform your perception of success. The more you celebrate your wins, the more your brain associates success with happiness, leading to a delightful spiral of achievement and joy—like an endless loop of your favorite song, but with less dancing and more productivity (unless dancing *is* your productivity, then go for it!).

Finally, remember that celebrating your wins isn't just about you. It's **contagious**! When you take the time to acknowledge your successes, you inspire those around you to do the same. Imagine a workplace filled with people who cheer each other on like they're at a championship game. It's a win-win situation. So, go ahead and throw that confetti (real or imaginary), treat yourself to something special, and share your victories with others. After all, in the grand scheme of life, if you don't celebrate your wins, you might just end up as a grumpy cat in a world full of sunny puppies. And nobody wants that! You've put in the effort, you've learned, you've grown. Give yourself credit where credit is due – you're a work in progress, and that progress deserves applause.

Pause & Ponder: Your Victory Vault

It's time to build your own personal vault of triumphs!

1 List Your Top 3 Recent Wins (Big or Small): Seriously, no win is too tiny. Did you send that difficult email? Did you stick to your budget for the week? Did you finally organize your desktop? Did you breathe deeply instead of reacting impatiently? Write them down.

2 How Did You Feel? What emotions did you experience when you achieved these wins? (e.g., proud, relieved, excited, calm, competent).

3 Your Celebration Method: For each win, decide how you'll celebrate. It doesn't have to be grand.

◦ *Examples:* A mental high-five, a quick "victory dance" in your chair, a special treat, telling a trusted friend, writing it down in a "Win Journal."

4 Affirm Your Success: Create a short, celebratory affirmation for yourself that you can say when you achieve something.

◦ *Example:* "I am a consistent achiever, making progress one joyful step at a time!"

◦ *My version:* "Nailed it! My patience (or quick rebound from impatience) is becoming legendary. High five, brain!"

The Road Ahead: Keeping the Momentum

Maintaining Your Cool: Staying Empowered in Stressful Times (Because Life Doesn't Hand Out Participation Trophies for Panicking)

In the high-stakes world of business (and frankly, just *life*), where deadlines loom larger than a sumo wrestler in a phone booth, maintaining your cool might seem like an Olympic sport. Imagine that pivotal moment when your presentation is due, and your PowerPoint decides to take a vacation to the digital Bermuda Triangle. You could either scream, cry, or channel your inner Zen master while silently affirming, "I am calm, cool, and collected, even if my software is having a mid-life crisis." Spoiler alert: the latter option will get you a lot further than flailing your arms like a windmill in a hurricane. Just remember, maintaining your composure is like juggling flaming torches—impressive when you pull it off, but not so much when you drop one on your boss's new shoes. For someone like me, the internal struggle often boils down to: "I want this fixed *now*! Why isn't it fixed *now*?! Must... resist... yelling at the monitor!"

The magic of self-talk comes into play like a trusty sidekick in a buddy cop movie. When chaos threatens to turn your brain into a blender on high speed, hit the brakes with some positive affirmations. It's like having your own motivational DJ spinning tracks that say, "You've got this!" and "Breathe in confidence, exhale anxiety!" So, next time you feel the pressure mounting like a three-tier cake at a wedding, just remind yourself that you're the master of your fate and the captain of your cool. Besides, a little humor can go a long way; after all, who doesn't want to be the person who cracks a joke while everyone else is sweating bullets?

Now, let's talk about the art of the **power pose**. You know, that super-heroic stance that makes you feel like you could bench-press a small car? Stand tall, shoulders back, and strike a pose that says, "I'm ready for anything!" Bonus points if you do this in front of a mirror while chanting affirmations like "I am stronger than my coffee addiction!" or "I can handle whatever this day throws at me, even if it's a surprise meeting with my ex-boss." The key here is to trick your brain into believing you are the embodiment of calmness, even if internally you're channeling a cat stuck in a bathtub. Studies show that these physical postures can actually influence your hormone levels, decreasing cortisol and increasing testosterone, literally making you feel more powerful and less stressed. So, go ahead, strike a pose!

Of course, there will always be those days when the universe seems determined to test your patience. Maybe your colleague spills coffee on your important documents, or the Wi-Fi decides to play hide-and-seek just as you're about to close the biggest deal of your career. In these moments, remember to take a deep breath and deploy your favorite catchphrase. Something like "This too shall pass" works wonders, especially if you say it with the seriousness of a philosopher contemplating the meaning of life. A little humor mixed with self-talk can lighten the mood and remind you that you're not alone in this circus. My internal self-talk during such moments often sounds like: "Okay, brain, this is not the time for panic. This is the time for... a plan. A *calm* plan.

Even if the plan involves a small, contained scream into a pillow later."

Strategic Stress Management: Proactive vs. Reactive

Maintaining your cool isn't just about reacting brilliantly in the moment; it's also about setting yourself up for success proactively.

• **Stress Inoculation (Mental Practice):** Just like a vaccine prepares your body for a virus, you can prepare your mind for stress. Think about an upcoming stressful event. Mentally walk through it, anticipating potential challenges, and then practice your calm, cool, and collected self-talk responses. Visualize yourself breathing deeply, using "I" statements, and even finding humor in the situation. The more you "practice" calmly in your mind, the better you'll perform when the real pressure hits.

• **Energy Management (Beyond Caffeine):** You can't be calm, cool, and collected if you're running on empty. Prioritize sleep, even when deadlines loom. Fuel your body with nutritious food (not just emergency chocolate). And find time for physical activity, even if it's just a brisk walk. These aren't luxuries; they're essential foundations for mental resilience. My own impatience often leads me to skip meals or cut sleep, thinking it saves time. It never does. It only makes me a grumpier, less effective version of myself.

• **Setting Boundaries (The "No Thanks" Power):** Sometimes, staying cool means gracefully saying "no." Saying no to extra commitments, saying no to negativity, saying no to distractions that derail your calm. Protecting your time and energy is a powerful act of self-care that prevents overwhelm.

Finally, let's not forget the importance of a solid support system. Surround yourself with people who can keep you laughing when stress tries to turn you into a grumpy cat. Friends and colleagues who appreciate your quirks and can share a laugh during tough times are invaluable. When the going gets tough, it's nice to know you have a crew ready to remind you that you're not just a business person but a superhero in disguise. So, keep those affirmations and good vibes flowing, and you'll find that staying empowered in stressful times isn't just a goal—it's a lifestyle choice, preferably with a side of laughter.

Pause & Ponder: Your Stress Survival Kit

1 Identify a Recurring Stressor: What's one specific thing that consistently makes you lose your cool or feel overwhelmed? (e.g., tight deadlines, micromanagement, conflict, feeling unheard, traffic jams).

2 Proactive Self-Talk: Before you next face this stressor, craft a humorous and empowering self-talk statement or affirmation you can use.

◦ *Example for tight deadlines:* "I am a deadline demolition expert, crushing goals with focus and a calm smile (and maybe a little bit of magic)."

◦ *My version for traffic:* "This is a perfect opportunity to practice extreme patience. I'm choosing to channel the inner calm of a sloth enjoying a long nap."

3 Choose a "Cool-Down" Strategy: What one practical step (breathing, power pose, mindful moment) can you commit to doing *during* or immediately *after* this stressor?

4 Embrace the Imperfect: If you *do* lose your cool, how will you use humor and self-compassion to get back on track? (e.g., "Well, that was a fiery moment! Time for a deep breath and a gentle re-entry into the atmosphere of calm.")

The Journey Is the Destination: Enjoying the Ride (Because Life's Too Short for Just Staring at the GPS)

In the grand adventure of life, we often find ourselves so focused on the destination that we forget to enjoy the ride. Think of life as a road trip with your favorite playlist, but instead of singing along, you're glued to the GPS, nervously calculating your ETA, convinced that every red light is a personal affront. My own impatient brain is notorious for this: "Are we there yet? No? But we *should* be! What's the fastest route? Can we bypass this scenic detour?"

Sure, you want to reach your goals, but if you don't take time to appreciate the scenery, you might end up missing the quirky roadside attractions—like that giant ball of yarn or the world's largest rubber band ball. These delightful detours can be just the spark you need to ignite your creativity and keep your sanity intact. The "destination" is often fleeting, but the "journey" is where all the living, learning, and laughing actually happens.

Let's take a moment to reflect on the fact that the journey is often more entertaining than the destination itself. Remember that time you planned a perfect vacation but ended up getting gloriously lost, discovering a hidden gem of a diner that served pancakes the size of your car? Those moments, my friends, are what give life its zest. Instead of fixating on your end goal, take a cue from those unexpected detours. Embrace the chaos, and when things go awry, laugh it off. A little humor can turn a frustrating moment into a memorable story, and in the business world, those stories are often more valuable than the actual results. They build character, and sometimes, a legendary reputation for being unflappable (or at least, hilariously flappable, but with quick recovery).

Now, let's talk about self-talk. It's the inner voice that can either be your biggest cheerleader or your worst critic. Imagine if that voice was a witty travel guide instead. Instead of saying, "I'll never make that deadline, this is impossible," how about, "Look at me, racing against time like a caffeinated tortoise on roller skates – and enjoying the wind in my metaphorical hair!" Positive affirmations can transform your inner dialogue into a source of amusement and motivation. So, the next time you find yourself stressing over deadlines or meetings, channel your inner comedian and turn those anxious thoughts into punchlines. Laughter is a natural stress reliever, and it's hard to feel overwhelmed when you're chuckling at your own absurdity.

Mindful Meandering: The Art of Present Moment Awareness

To truly enjoy the ride, you need to practice **mindful mean-**

dering. This isn't about aimless wandering; it's about purposefully paying attention to the present moment, even (especially!) the mundane ones.

• **The Coffee Moment:** Don't just drink your coffee. Taste it. Feel the warmth of the mug. Notice the aroma. For those few seconds, that's your entire world.

• **The Commute Chronicle:** Instead of fuming about traffic, notice the sky, the trees, the funny bumper sticker on the car in front of you. My impatient self finds this particularly challenging, but even a few seconds of observation can break the cycle of frustration.

• **The Meeting Minute:** Instead of mentally checking out, truly listen to one person. Notice their expressions, their tone. Be fully present for just a minute.

These small acts of mindfulness anchor you to the "now," preventing your mind from constantly racing ahead to the next task or dwelling on past regrets. They help you appreciate the journey itself, not just the destination.

As you navigate the twists and turns of your professional journey, remember that every bump in the road has the potential to teach you something valuable. Picture yourself as a seasoned traveler who has learned to pack light, ditch the unnecessary baggage (like excessive worry and self-criticism), and savor the experience. When you approach challenges with a sense of humor, you'll discover that setbacks can be springboards for growth. Instead of sulking over a missed opportunity, laugh at the irony and think, "Well, that was a plot twist worthy of a sitcom, and I'm ready for the next season!" This shift in perspective can turn even the most mundane situations into learning experiences.

Ultimately, the key to thriving in both business and everyday life lies in your ability to enjoy the ride. Embrace the unpredictable, let go of perfection, and remember that it's okay to laugh at yourself. Life is too short to be serious all the time, so why not find joy in the journey? The next time you feel the pressure mounting, take a moment to pause, crack a smile, and remind yourself that sometimes, the best destination is simply the one you're currently traveling. After all, the only thing better than reaching your goals is having a good laugh along the way, and realizing that being **Cool Under Pressure, Warm with Humor** is not just a goal, but a wonderfully chaotic, consistently evolving way of life.

Final Pause & Ponder: Your Ongoing Adventure

1 Your Personal "Roadside Attraction": What's one small, everyday moment or activity that you can commit to experiencing more mindfully this week, simply for the joy of the "journey"? (e.g., your morning coffee, a walk, a conversation with a loved one, a specific task at work).

2 Your Humorous Life Motto: Based on everything we've discussed, what's a short, funny, and empowering motto that encapsulates your approach to staying calm, cool, and collected in this ongoing adventure?

° *Example:* "My life is a perfectly imperfect comedy, and I'm the star who always finds the punchline."

° *My motto:* "I'm learning to slow down and smell the roses, even if I'm still internally calculating the most efficient path through the rose garden."

3 The Continuous Journey: Remember that this isn't a "one-and-done" book. It's a toolkit for life. Revisit these pages, practice the techniques, and keep finding the humor in your journey. You've got this!

About the Author

George Hatcher is a man who has always believed that the world is full of opportunities waiting for those bold enough to seize them. With a ninth-grade education and a wealth of unique experiences, he has faced the ups and downs of life head-on. At the age of 20, while serving time, George took the initiative to complete the assignments and tests necessary to earn his high school diploma. His own life is a treasure trove of stories waiting to be uncovered.

Over the years, George has enjoyed a diverse career as an entrepreneur, consultant, and strategist. He has served as a peacemaker for athletes and their parents, as well as a crisis management advisor for physicians and attorneys, achieving considerable success in client development and public relations. He is a licensed boxing manager in California, though he currently has no boxers signed.

George has logged over 200,000 air miles annually through business travel and pleasure trips with his wife. However, since the onset of COVID-19 in 2020, his travel has come to a halt. Now, in retirement, George finds that life remains an ongoing adventure. Unfortunately, he is fighting several new battles that he never anticipated, yet he continues to discover something new with each step.

As a passionate storyteller, George has published a dozen books and finds immense joy in writing. With the world opening up again, he has seized the opportunity to immerse himself fully in his literary pursuits. He currently resides in Rancho Mirage, California, with his wife, Molly, his partner for 59 years, and their home is filled with three cats and two macaws. Each experience in his life has taught him invaluable lessons about adaptability, perseverance, and a touch of luck. Like the person who hits their head just to feel the pleasure of stopping, George has made his share of mistakes—some more than once. He hopes others can learn from them as he has.

Now devoted entirely to writing, George Hatcher invites others to join him on this remarkable journey, filled with lessons and stories that showcase the beauty of life's unpredictability.

A longer bio is on his website at
http://georgehatcher.com/bio/bio.html

www.ingramcontent.com/pod-product-compliance
Lightning Source LLC
Chambersburg PA
CBHW061708120626
46550CB00003B/1140